insight text guide

Sue Sherman

Inheritance

Hannie Rayson

insight®

▶ innovative ▶ engaging ▶ evolving

First published in 2005, reprinted in 2020.

Insight Publications Pty Ltd
3/350 Charman Road
Cheltenham VIC 3192
Australia
Tel: +61 3 8571 4950
Fax: +61 3 8571 0257
Email: books@insightpublications.com.au

www.insightpublications.com.au

National Library of Australia Cataloguing-in-Publication entry:
Sherman, Sue, 1946-
Hannie Rayson's Inheritance : text guide.
For VCE English students.
ISBN 9781921088018 (paperback).
1. Rayson, Hannie, 1957 – Inheritance. I. Title.
A 822.3

Other ISBNs:
9781922378910 (digital)
9781922378927 (bundle: print + digital)

Cover design by Gisela Beer

Printed in Australia by Ligare

contents

Character map iv

Introduction 1

Context & background 3

Genre, style & structure 9

Scene-by-scene analysis 16

Characters & relationships 40

Themes, ideas & values 55

Questions & answers 66

Sample answer 71

References & reading 74

CHARACTER MAP

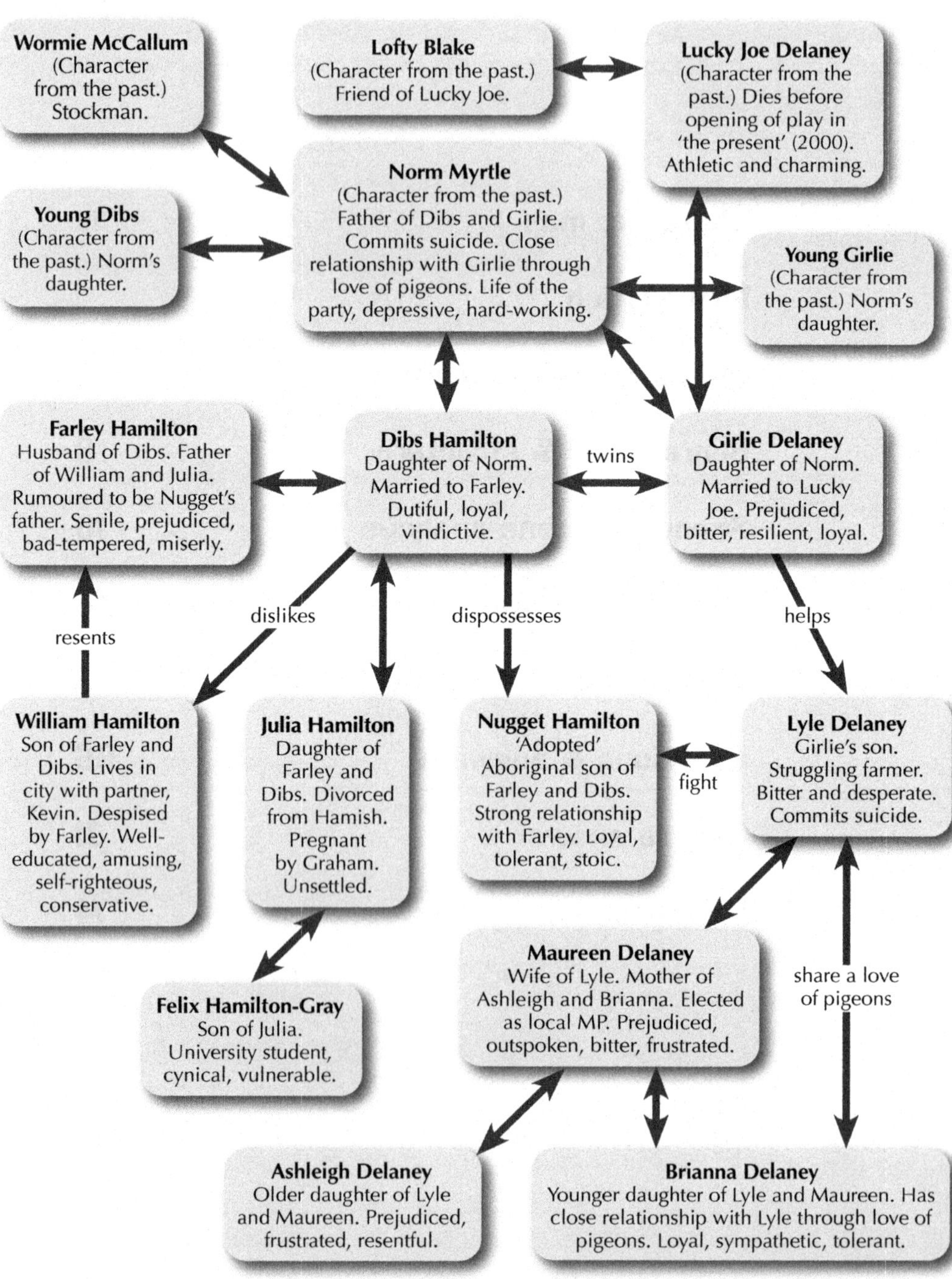

INTRODUCTION

Since graduating from the Victorian College of the Arts, Hannie Rayson has become one of Australia's most influential playwrights. *Hotel Sorrento* (1990), one of her early plays, has been made into a successful film, while *Life After George* (2000) followed its acclaimed Melbourne production with a short season in London's famous West End theatre district.

Inheritance, like Rayson's other plays, examines individuals and families under pressure as they cope with dramatic change. In the two-and-a-half years it took to write *Inheritance*, Rayson visited the Mallee town of Nyah West and its surroundings ten times. Having lived most of her life in Melbourne, Rayson used her visits to the Mallee to gain an insight into why rural people were so supportive of the controversial conservative politics of Pauline Hanson and One Nation.[1] What she discovered was a community struggling to cope with the enduring effects of the rural recession.

In the Mallee, as in all rural communities, farmers have traditionally enjoyed the privileged position of being essential to Australia's economy because they controlled the nation's primary resources. For a long time, government policies protected the interests of farmers, but this changed radically with the shift to economic rationalism, which was seen by many farmers as a betrayal. Suddenly, farmers were confronted with debt, mouse plagues, droughts, price collapses, Aboriginal land claims and crippling foreign competition.[2] In response, many country people turned their backs on the government, and some saw Pauline Hanson, with her rural origins and plain-speaking appeals to 'common sense', as a saviour.

Rayson's sympathetic response to the plight of country people is evident in her gritty, endearing and vulnerable characters. She does not refrain from exposing bitterness, greed and prejudice; however, nor

---

[1] Robin Usher, 'Hannie's outback odyssey', The Age, 21 February 2003, The Culture p.3.

[2] Rosalyn Darracott, Applying a grief model to working with pastoralists, National Rural Health Alliance, 2003, https://eprints.qut.edu.au/101410/1/darracott.pdf

does *Inheritance* suggest that country people are any more prejudiced than their city neighbours are, and fictional Rushton can be seen as a microcosm of the larger political landscape. As the Hamiltons and Delaneys battle over the inheritance of the family farm, larger questions loom about Aboriginal land rights, the stolen generations, immigration, race and the complex relationship between legal rights and moral rights.

In considering questions about our rights and responsibilities as individuals and as citizens, we are also urged to think about our inheritance – in a broad sense – in terms of what we take from the past, and what we pass on to future generations. Is inheritance a curse or a blessing? How are we shaped by our cultural, political and genetic inheritance? Do some inherited cultural traditions deliberately exclude newcomers? In this short play about a twentieth-century Australian family, Rayson explores some of the issues which have preoccupied the nation since white settlement, and which are still largely unresolved.

CONTEXT & BACKGROUND

Economic factors

Q Why were farmers like Lyle Delaney in such desperate financial trouble in the late 1990s?

There are several reasons for this. To begin with, during the 1980s and 1990s rural Australia experienced a series of catastrophic events, which precipitated what came to be called the 'rural recession' and adversely affected almost everyone who lived in a country town. Many farmers had been unwise, thinking that the good times of the previous decade would continue. Most had borrowed heavily, failing to keep money in reserve in the event of disasters such as those that occurred in the 1980s, including:

- natural disasters – in 1999, the NSW Parliament referred to the 1982–83 drought as the worst ever experienced
- economic factors such as
  - the steady rise in interest rates during the 1980s
  - the collapse in the 'floor price' of wool
  - the decline in lamb sales in the face of competition from beef
  - the removal of the 'guaranteed' minimum price for wheat.

During the 1980s, interest rates and inflation were already at record highs. Moreover, the harmful effects of these factors were exacerbated by a taxation system that encouraged businesses (including farms) to have a high level of borrowings.

Deregulation

When the Hawke Government deregulated the banking industry, the banks were able to lend a higher proportion of a valuation. This led to increased competition between the banks and it became easier to borrow money. The banks lent larger sums of money than had previously been possible without taking into account the borrower's ability to repay the loan. Farmers were placed in a difficult position, needing to borrow large sums of money to keep their farms productive and having to pay high interest rates on the money they borrowed. Spiralling debt rapidly became a vicious circle from which there was no escape.[3]

Psychological strains

> Believing that they were a financial drain on the family, some children approached school counsellors to find out how they could be adopted or fostered out. The severe psychological strain on children sometimes led to suicide attempts. They would hear their parents arguing about the fact they may lose the farm which meant that they would also lose their homes. They would hear their fathers, particularly, talking about burning the place, burning the bank, shooting the bank manager or shooting themselves.[4]

Many farm families felt a sense of helplessness and anger about their financial situation – in *Inheritance*, the Delaney family certainly falls into this category. Rural communities believed that they had lost control of their lives; their self-esteem and confidence evaporated. Country people also felt neglected, harbouring a sense of betrayal by authorities.[5] Maureen Delaney's appeals to the anger and despair of the locals strike a deep chord (p.61), just as Pauline Hanson's did in the 1996 federal election (see below under 'The rise of Pauline Hanson and One Nation').

Banks and economic rationalism

As well as making it clear that farmers like Lyle Delaney were partly responsible for their own financial mismanagement, Rayson invites her audience to consider the moral responsibility of institutions such

[3] Social Development Committee of the Parliament of South Australia, *Rural poverty in South Australia: interim report of the Social Development Committee*, Parliament of South Australia, 1994, p.16, http://www.parliament.sa.gov.au/committees/lccdocuments/SD/public_documents/Tabled%20Reports/04th%20Report;%20Interim%20Rural%20Poverty%20Inquiry%20Report.pdf (no longer available)

[4] *Rural poverty in South Australia*, p.18.

[5] *Rural poverty in South Australia*, p.22.

as banks. In particular, banks have been criticised for being too willing to lend money to those who cannot afford to repay, eventually seizing their properties and leaving them homeless and destitute – which is what happens to the Delaneys in *Inheritance*. This brand of economic rationalism is driven by the ruthless demands of the market. Banks make large profits for shareholders. According to the underlying assumptions of economic rationalism, this is 'good for the economy' since it creates strong employment and investor and consumer confidence. However, critics of economic rationalism argue that such practices exhibit a callous disregard for individuals, like Lyle Delaney, who get into financial difficulties.

Political background

An understanding of the following political factors will give you greater insight into the background of the play, even though they are not directly responsible for the problems experienced by farming communities.

Eddie Mabo

Edward Koiki Mabo was born in 1936 on the island of Mer, one of the Murray Islands, which are located at the eastern extremity of Torres Strait. In June 1992, six months after his death, Mabo achieved national prominence as the successful principal plaintiff in the landmark High Court ruling on native land title. The High Court ruling gave, for the first time, legal recognition to the fact that Indigenous land ownership existed in Australia before European settlement.[6]

Aboriginal land rights

When Europeans arrived on the Australian continent, they stepped from their ships onto land which was owned under complex Indigenous laws and land systems. However, it has taken white Australia and its legal system more than two hundred years to acknowledge this fact. Despite

[6] Biographical notes on Eddie Mabo are provided on the website *Papers of Edward Koiki Mabo*, National Library of Australia, https://nla.gov.au/nla.obj-224065802/findingaid

the dislocation that has occurred since 1788, traditional Aboriginal laws and customs governing land ownership have continued to survive in much of Australia to varying degrees and in various forms. Even where families move away from their 'country', their connections can survive their absence. Nugget Hamilton, the 'adopted' Aboriginal son of Dibs and Farley Hamilton, symbolises all dispossessed Indigenous peoples. Felix Hamilton-Gray recognises this when he asserts that Nugget should inherit the farm because: 'His people have already been dispossessed once' (p.91).

The land rights struggle

Indigenous people have been fighting for their land since 1788. In the late 1960s, when the Gurindji walked off Wave Hill cattle station over their appalling work conditions, they drew national attention to the struggle. The *Racial Discrimination Act 1975* and the Woodward Royal Commission report laid the basis for Commonwealth land rights legislation in the Northern Territory in 1975. Land rights legislation in some of the states followed. Although these statutes granted some land rights to many Aboriginal people, Australian law still did not recognise prior Indigenous ownership of Australian land. It was not until 1992, in the historic Mabo decision, that Australian law acknowledged the legal force and validity of Indigenous land claims.

The stolen generations

From the end of the nineteenth century to the late twentieth century – the dates are uncertain – Australian governments removed Aboriginal children from their mothers, parents, families and communities, often by force. Some of these children were taken at birth, some at two years of age, some in their childhood years. The babies and children were sent either to special-purpose institutions or to foster homes. In some cases, mothers or families knew where their children had been taken and were able to maintain some continuing connection with them. In other cases, they had no idea of their children's whereabouts. In some cases the children were treated well in the institutions and the foster homes, although even here, it would appear, frequently with condescension. In other cases, physical mistreatment, sexual exploitation and other extreme forms of humiliation were common.[7]

In *Inheritance*, Nugget symbolises the stolen generations. While in some respects he is treated well – just as some Aboriginal children were in similar circumstances – colonial condescension and paternalism remain. He is sent to Longerenong Agricultural College while the legitimate white heir, William, attends an elite city boarding school. Dibs assumes, as many of her colonial predecessors did, that she and Farley are fulfilling their 'Christian' duty in offering Nugget 'advantages' that his Aboriginal family cannot provide. Yet despite her knowledge of his parentage, Dibs asserts that Nugget is 'not family' (p.77). Moreover, he is expected to be 'grateful' (p.76) for the favours bestowed on him by his white benefactors. Ultimately, Nugget (whose nickname appals Felix with its racist connotations) is little more than an unpaid labourer on a farm he will not inherit.

The rise of Pauline Hanson and One Nation

Pauline Hanson was a member of the Liberal Party, and from 1994 to 1996 she was a local councillor in the Queensland city of Ipswich.[8] She was endorsed as the Liberal candidate for the electorate of Oxley for the March 1996 federal election. However, comments that Hanson made to *The Queensland Times*, in which she advocated the abolition of special government assistance for Aboriginal people, led to her disendorsement by the party during the campaign. As a result, Hanson campaigned for and won the seat of Oxley as an independent.

In September 1996, Hanson made her maiden speech to the House of Representatives, which instantly made headlines and the television news bulletins across Australia. She expressed her concern that Australia was 'in danger of being swamped by Asians', and generally decried many aspects of what she labelled as 'political correctness'.

---

[7] Robert Manne, *The Stolen Generations: Robert Manne's essay*, Tim Richardson, 1998, http://tim-richardson.net/index.php/opinion/the-stolen-generations-robert-manne

[8] These and the following comments about Pauline Hanson are sourced from the online article *Pauline Hanson*, http://en.wikipedia.org/wiki/Pauline_Hanson

As a result of her maiden speech, Hanson became a very controversial figure, with the Australian population divided on whether she was honest and plain-spoken (a view more likely to be held in regional areas), a dangerous racist, or a misinformed yokel. Hanson's critics derided what they saw as her inarticulate style – the very trait that her supporters took to be evidence of her credentials as a speaker 'for the people'. Subsequently, Hanson and her supporters established the One Nation political party, which included the following statement as part of its immigration policy:

> Inappropriately high levels of immigration combined with the policy of multiculturalism has led to a serious breakdown in the social cohesion of Australia.[9]

Rejection of the 'outsider' is evident in the attitudes of several characters in *Inheritance*.

[9] Cited by Sarah Peckham, *Pauline Hanson & One Nation*, Action for Aboriginal Rights, 1998, http://home.vicnet.net.au/~aar/sarah2.htm (no longer available).

GENRE, STYLE & STRUCTURE

Genre: drama

The basic point of all plays in both formal and thematic terms is that characters are always 'caught up in some sort of crisis, dilemma or confusion'.[10] A useful starting point for the discussion of a play is an awareness of the issue or problem it is concerned with. All plays:

> employ the same basic structure of exposition, complication and resolution. With this in mind, the similarity between *all* plays, be they Greek or Shakespearean tragedy or modern drama, becomes apparent.[11]

Plays are different from novels and poems in that they are intended for public performance and tend to focus on 'public questions of the social and political organisation of society'.[12] Rayson's play certainly does this. The central section of a play, in which confusion reigns, begins 'to raise questions about the whole social order'.[13] As problems develop and 'the characters begin to find themselves in unfamiliar and uncomfortable predicaments, we are forced to consider how precarious the social order is – and how close we always are to disorder'.[14]

Other ways of reading the genre of *Inheritance*

Family drama

Family relationships come into conflict as tensions between generations erupt over issues of inheritance. The bonds that unite families (blood ties, shared values, loyalty, love and duty) are strained to breaking point.

---

[10] John Peck & Martin Coyle, *Literary Terms and Criticism*, Macmillan, London, 1984, p.75.

[11] Peck & Coyle, *Literary Terms and Criticism*, p.75.

[12] Peck & Coyle, *Literary Terms and Criticism*, p.75.

[13] Peck & Coyle, *Literary Terms and Criticism*, p.75.

[14] Peck & Coyle, *Literary Terms and Criticism*, pp.75–6.

Social commentary

Significant economic and political events of the 1980s are critically examined. While land rights and the stolen generations were at the forefront of political discussion, the rural recession deepened and interest rates soared. These economic factors exacerbated tensions felt over land-right issues. With their lives thrown into turmoil, white rural families like the Delaneys succumbed to debt and despair.

Comedy

Elements of slapstick, black humour and even farce pervade some of the scenes, particularly those involving the most eccentric characters Girlie and Farley – both ageing, irascible and often comically uncompromising. The play's coarse language is also often highly amusing, as is some of the 'politically incorrect' dialogue between Maureen and Girlie.

Tragedy

As comic elements begin to take on a darker edge, a dramatic shift from comedy to tragedy intensifies the play's increasingly ominous tone. Lyle Delaney, the tragic hero, bears a striking resemblance to his grandfather, Norm Myrtle, whose dreadful fate he shares.

Allegory

Recalling the history of white settlement in Australia, the Myrtle family history begins with pioneering Jessie Allan. Her family dispossesses the original inhabitants, develops the land and prospers. Alluding to another dark chapter in our history, the story of Joyce, Nugget's mother, highlights the tragedy of the stolen generations. Joyce is employed in a menial job and, like countless other Aboriginal girls who were raped or seduced by white men, Joyce becomes pregnant. Her son is adopted by a white family and effectively becomes an unpaid labourer.

The play also draws attention to current Aboriginal land rights claims. In the real world of Australian society as well as in the fictional world of the play, conservative, right-wing individuals respond to these claims with alarm and many endorse the politics of racism.[15] Maureen condemns 'do-gooders from the city [who peddle] tribal oogy-boogy' and Girlie scornfully dismisses the claims of the 'bloody Mabo mob' (pp.38–9). Yet Maureen adamantly asserts that there's 'nothing racist about [her] policies', arguing that concessions constitute 'extra privileges' (p.84). The similarities with Pauline Hanson's comments in *The Queensland Times* are not coincidental. Just as Hanson was, Maureen is elected as an independent.

Australian literature

Set in rural Victoria, in a landscape that is recognisably Australian, *Inheritance* explores ideas about being Australian and asks audiences to reflect on what that might mean. Rayson has explained that she wanted to 'take audiences outside the mainstream into other worlds that inform us about who we are as Australians'.[16] The characters – the pioneer (Jessie Allan, Dibs and Girlie's grandmother); the 'squatter' (Norm Myrtle); the battler (Lyle Delaney); the larrikin (Lucky Joe Delaney); the Aboriginal 'stockman' (Nugget) – are archetypal Australian figures. Dibs and Girlie are gritty outback women – the 'backbone' of their respective families; Maureen Delaney is one of a new breed of country women: a farmer's wife who is politicised by adversity. Yet the characters emerge as strong individuals and are much more complex than these labels would suggest.

Postcolonial text

Inheritance demands an awareness of the effects of colonisation on a nation's inhabitants, both Indigenous and settler. During the period of European colonialism (roughly 1400–1945), colonial powers positioned the colonised peoples and places as 'the other', in the sense that they were perceived to be 'alien, non-Western and therefore inferior'.[17] In Australia, this 'inferiority' was considered a sufficient justification for

---

[15] A left-wing response at this time by Phillip Adams was published in *The Weekend Australian Magazine* on 23–4 July 2005, p.46.

[16] Usher, 'Hannie's outback odyssey'.

[17] Christopher O'Reilly, *Context in Literature: Post Colonial Literature*, Cambridge University Press, Cambridge, 2001, p.106.

the dispossession and gradual extermination of thousands of Aboriginal people and for the erosion of their culture.

Rayson also observes and condemns xenophobic responses to multiculturalism, driven by outdated notions of Anglo-Saxon racial superiority. As the Hamiltons and the Delaneys squabble about who Allandale belongs to, larger questions loom in the background about who Australia belongs to, and who belongs in Australia.

Feminist text

Inheritance is a critique of a historical patriarchy in that it makes explicit the ways in which gender, class and race act as barriers to equality when power is in the hands of an elite group of dominant men. Rayson's play shows how some of the patriarchal power structures of the Old World were perpetuated in the colonies. In staking their claim to 'new' lands, colonists relied on mateship, resourcefulness and resilience, and showed a healthy disrespect for unjust authority. The very notion of Australianness came to be linked to such qualities and has been perpetuated in our cultural archetypes: the explorer, the swagman, the stockman, the squatter, the bushranger, the digger, the bronzed surfer, and the sporting hero – all of which are exclusively or predominantly masculine.

In rethinking Australian identity, Rayson creates strong, assertive and enterprising female characters, like Jessie Allan (who is also a coloniser) and her granddaughters, Dibs and Girlie Myrtle. Unlike their male counterparts, however, these characters do not escape the negative implications of participating in a colonising tradition.

Elements of style

Language

Rayson's characters are mostly plain-speaking, country people. Their language, developed from eighteenth-century British criminal slang, was transported with the convicts to antipodean penal settlements. As the colony became gentrified, the Old World class distinctions were preserved in the differences between the 'Queen's English' of the ruling classes and the slang of the convicts and their descendants. The colourful language of the 'lower class' colonists expressed an anti-authoritarian attitude which came to be seen as quintessentially Australian.

This class distinction is noted in Maureen Delaney's reference to the Hamiltons' 'private school voices' (p.38). Rayson's script is littered with colloquial Australian expressions such as 'grog' (p.9), 'stoushed' (p.9), 'completely ga-ga' (p.37), 'sheilas' (p.42), 'a bit of all right' (p.42) and 'a great bloke' (p.45), as well as a liberal (and characteristically Australian) use of coarse and mildly blasphemous language. In the voices of her characters, Rayson captures the cadences of a uniquely Australian vernacular.

Humour

Rayson's humour is also typically Australian: in the opening scene, for example, humour is wry and self-deprecating, downplaying any suggestion of self-importance with props like a 'sheep's head' trophy. In the early scenes, much of the humour is derived from the coarseness of the language and the comic effects of props such as the motorised lawnmower and the 'exploding' Toyota Corolla. Unsophisticated country characters are also traditionally a source of humour for city audiences; Dibs' attempt to pronounce 'focaccias' (p.26), for example, offers city dwellers like William Hamilton a reassuring sense of urban 'superiority'.

In a similar vein, Girlie's racist sentiments are amusing because they are so blatantly politically incorrect and because she is essentially a comic character whose views can be more easily dismissed. Many city dwellers such as Julia, who consider themselves more sophisticated and politically sensitive, might not *say* such things, but might unconsciously endorse (as Julia does) some of these politically incorrect sentiments. The humour begins to veer uncomfortably offcourse, however, as Maureen transforms eccentric bigotry into a political agenda. The line between what is amusing and what is offensive, Rayson suggests, is often an uncomfortably blurred one.

Alienation

Another important stylistic feature is a Brechtian element in the play.[18] This is immediately evident in the prologue as the actors 'gaze into the auditorium ... as though watching strangers coming into town' (p.1). By engaging directly with the audience, the actors detach themselves from the characters. This breaks down the theatrical 'fourth wall'.[19] It is a (now familiar) Brechtian device whereby the play deliberately unsettles audience expectations about theatrical conventions, drawing attention to itself as something constructed. In preventing the audience from completely 'losing' themselves in the story of the play, the playwright forces viewers to think about 'the more abstract, political questions raised'.[20]

Structure

Inheritance is a two-act play, beginning in the past and shifting constantly between the past and the present. Boundaries between past and present often dissolve entirely as the living and the dead characters speak to each other across the temporal divide. This structural device dramatically highlights the enduring effects of the past, which quite literally intrudes at significant moments. The flashback to Norm and Girlie's releasing of the pigeons parallels a similar event with Lyle and Brianna two generations later, emphasising the grim inevitability of Lyle's fate.

In the early scenes the mood is comic but, as Act one unfolds, it becomes increasingly tense; more of the family arrives for Dibs and Girlie's eightieth birthdays and unresolved family issues darken the

[18] This term derives from the plays and philosophy of the German dramatist, Bertolt Brecht (1899–1956). Brecht sought to disrupt the audience's immersion in the play's narrative through a process known as 'alienation'. 'Alienating' techniques in *Inheritance* include the frequent interruption of action and dialogue, and unsettling music.

[19] The term fourth wall 'applies to the imaginary invisible wall at the front of the stage in a theatre through which the audience sees the action' ('Fourth Wall', http://en.wikipedia.org/wiki/Fourth_wall). In *Inheritance*, the breaking down of this fourth wall is both humorous and alienating.

[20] Peck & Coyle, *Literary Terms and Criticism*, p.89.

mood. The action of the drama unfolds through short but often very intense scenes. Humour is juxtaposed with drama and tragedy through rapid scene changes which cut between the Hamiltons and Delaneys, charting the disintegration of their relationships. Sometimes it seems as if the action lurches (as Lyle Delaney does) almost out of control, from one scene to another. The cumulative effect of these dramatic shifts and rapid cuts is to increase the tension, culminating in the powerful climax at the end of Act one and the fulfilment of Lyle's tragic destiny in Act two.

The sound of the church choir also functions as a structural device, calling up the past or intruding into the present. In Act one, scene twenty, the 'dissonant and unhinged' music reflects the emotional state of Norm Myrtle and introduces a moment of dramatic irony (p.34). The words of the Christmas carol, 'Away in a Manger' (p.35), with its message of hope, are juxtaposed with fragments of dialogue from the prologue and the girls' gruesome discovery of their father 'swinging from the rafters' (p.35).

The play builds to a shocking climax at the end of Act one, followed by a dramatic 'Blackout' (p.58) which signals the act's end and symbolises the chaos and despair that has engulfed Lyle Delaney. Act two begins as abruptly as Act one ends – with a shift in focus from the bitter family feud to the emergence of Maureen Delaney as a local political force. A humorous tone is briefly re-established as the family buries Farley, but it is very black humour and quickly dissipates.

At the close of Act two, scene seven, the words of 'Praise My Soul, the King of Heaven' provide another ironic contrast – this time in a darkly comic vein – as the hymn's Christian sentiments highlight the family's un-Christian behaviour (p.79).

Structurally, the rise of Maureen, the political opportunist, is set against the tragic demise of the disinherited pastoralists, while the dramatic swings – from comedy to tragedy to farce – highlight irresolvable tensions between the diametrically opposed forces that drive the narrative.

SCENE-BY-SCENE ANALYSIS

Prologue (pp.1–2)

Summary: *Set in 1934. Norm Myrtle, standing on his back verandah, welcomes the theatre audience as if they are part of a crowd scene within the play; Norm's young twin daughters sing 'Two Little Girls in Blue' as family and friends gather at Allandale for an annual ritual.*

The prologue introduces Norm Myrtle as the 'patriarch', a term synonymous with inherited power. Norm proudly introduces his daughters, Dibs and Girlie. The 'Norm Myrtle Memorial Trophy' – a sheep's skull adorned with a blue rosette (p.1) – emphasises (albeit ironically) the importance of family traditions and celebrates Norm's position as head of the family.

Act one, scene one (pp.3–4)

Summary: *Set in the present. Driving along an outback road, Julia Hamilton and her son, Felix, have broken down forty kilometres from the nearest town; Julia tries unsuccessfully to repair the car.*

This brief act humorously illustrates the helplessness of 'inner-city folk' (p.3) confronted by the uncompromising Australian outback. Julia's colourful language succinctly expresses her frustration. Humour arises not only from the utter irrationality of Julia's response, but also from her disapproval of Felix's use of the word she herself has just used seven times. The 'crow call', which repeats the sound of the word, is designed to evoke more laughter, but also seems to suggest that nature itself is mocking the stranded city visitors.

Scene two (pp.5–6)

Summary: *Dibs Hamilton and Girlie Delaney chat in the garden of the Hamiltons' farm. After arguing about the roses, Girlie leaves. Dibs expresses her regret at the breakdown of her daughter Julia's marriage to Hamish.*

Dibs introduces herself, addressing the audience directly and reinforcing the sense of intimacy between performers and spectators established in the prologue. Girlie dispenses unwanted advice on fertilising the roses and Dibs deals with Girlie's interference by agreeing, but not taking 'a jot of notice' (p.5). Their relationship, based on tolerance of each other's shortcomings, seems comfortable enough; however, Girlie still feels proprietorial about the garden. This reveals her unwillingness to relinquish her claim on the family property.

Scene three (pp.6–7)

Summary: *The Delaneys' house. The ramshackle appearance of the Delaney property suggests that Girlie has not done as well as Dibs. Lyle Delaney, Girlie's son, arrives with a motorised bike converted from a lawnmower – a gift for Girlie. Girlie is not impressed.*

This is another humorous scene: Lyle's mechanical expertise is used to great comic effect as he theatrically unveils the 'visual gag', but his moment of 'triumph' is humorously undercut by Girlie's description of his masterpiece as 'clapped out', 'a dead man's lawnmower' (p.6). Girlie's assertion that she does not want to look like 'the town idiot' (p.6) reveals her defensiveness about her physical disability. The typically 'Aussie' language – 'Don't be a piker' and the mildly blasphemous 'Jesus H. Christ' (p.7) – enhances the scene's humour, as does the slapstick effect of Girlie's undignified exit astride the ridiculous, noisy contraption. Even so, she is clearly not 'a piker', and this toughness is part of what sustains Girlie, even while it fuels her intolerance.

Scene four (p.7)

Summary: *The Hamiltons' farmhouse kitchen. William Hamilton arrives.*

The first four scenes provide an overview of family relationships in a society where property ownership and education provide access to power. William's arrival and his bantering tone with his mother suggest an easygoing relationship, although his teasing comments about her age might take on greater significance in the light of his plans to convince her to sell the farm.

Scene five (p.8)

Summary: *Still stranded on the Berriwillock Road, Julia and Felix wait for someone to rescue them. Julia tells Felix about some of her childhood experiences growing up in the Mallee.*

Structurally, this scene, with its demeaning reference to 'faggot races', is significantly placed immediately after the scene introducing William; offering a brief insight into the way homophobia has been naturalised in this community to the extent that it seems like harmless fun. It is ironic that Julia, with her disapproval of racial prejudice, is still 'amused by the memory'. Names such as 'Donger Maloney' reinforce the stereotyped values of a rather 'jockstrap' bush culture and predominantly Anglo-Irish heritage in which homophobic attitudes flourished.

Scene six (pp.8–9)

Summary: *Girlie enters on her motorised lawnmower and talks to Lyle about the forthcoming birthday celebrations.*

Girlie, now apparently quite happy to use her new motor, 'hoons across the stage' (p.8). The notion of an eighty-year-old woman 'hooning' on a motorised vehicle, let alone one which looks as ridiculous as Lyle's invention, is highly entertaining, but invites questions about whether Rayson is challenging or perpetuating stereotypical images of older people. This depends on whether we are expected to celebrate Girlie's indomitable spirit, or to enjoy, at Girlie's expense, the comic disjunction between an ageing woman and the youthful and masculine connotations of her mode of transport.

Scene seven (pp.9–11)

Summary: *In the kitchen at Allandale, Dibs makes sandwiches; Farley enters, converses briefly with Dibs then leaves, having barely acknowledged William.*

William's remark about Emu Barker who 'stoushed' (punched) him in primary school seems harmless at first, but William's memory of the incident has endured for over forty years. We are led to wonder if William was bullied in school because of his non-stereotypical masculinity. His assertion that 'gay men are not welcome in Rushton' (p.10), in response to Dibs' invitation to bring Kevin (p.9), makes explicit a homophobic element in the community. It also acknowledges the potential for violence which often accompanies homophobia, and which the 'faggot races' (p.8) attempt to disguise as harmless fun.

Scene eight (pp.11–12)

Summary: *Nugget answers the telephone call made by Dibs in the previous scene. He prepares to go to rescue Julia and Felix but, as he is leaving, he and Lyle argue about whether to buy a harvester or hire a contractor.*

As Nugget and Lyle argue about the wisdom of buying a harvester, it is clear that Lyle is frustrated and humiliated by his reliance on others. This scene reveals Lyle's bitterness at his lack of economic independence. The growing tension between Nugget and Lyle highlights fundamental differences in their characters and their approaches to farming – tensions which will escalate dramatically as the pressures on Lyle increase.

Scene nine (pp.12–13)

Summary: *Still stranded on the Berriwillock Road, Julia informs Felix that she is pregnant and that the father is an Indian colleague.*

Felix is rather taken aback by Julia's announcement; he thinks that Julia is 'a bit old', and seems surprised that she is 'planning to go ahead with [the] pregnancy' (p.13). He is also interested in whether Julia will tell her parents that she is going to have 'a little brown baby' (p.13). This reveals his awareness of his grandparents' racism, and perhaps unconsciously betrays some of his own prejudices lurking quietly beneath his left-wing, liberal politics.

Scene ten (pp.13–16)

Summary: *Girlie Delaney and her daughter-in-law, Maureen, walk down the main street of Rushton discussing the party and a range of family issues.*

Girlie is annoyed that Dibs has invited 'the wogs' to the party (p.13). Maureen reminds Girlie: 'Their boy put in a good game in the ruck last Saturday' (p.15). The importance of football in the local community, and their son's impressive ability, is perhaps the only path to acceptance for the Pappas family in Rushton. The focus of the conversation moves from racism to homophobia as Maureen reveals that she thought Felix, whose 'new girlfriend' is Japanese, was 'a homo' (p.15). Although Girlie's bias seems relatively harmless, even amusing perhaps, her prejudices reflect the values of a small but significant proportion of the Australian population who voted for Pauline Hanson's One Nation Party.

Scene eleven (pp.16–18)

Summary: *At the Hamiltons', William and Dibs carry in boxes for the party. They discuss Farley's deteriorating mental condition and William's plans to move him into appropriate accommodation. William wants Dibs to move to the Mornington Peninsula, where he and Kevin plan to set up a vineyard and restaurant.*

William tries to pin Dibs down by making an appointment with the social worker to discuss the options for Farley, but Dibs feels guilty about disregarding Farley's wish to be carried out of Allandale 'with me boots on' (p.11). She also feels gloomy about the prospect of having 'no friends', and concerned for Nugget, who will be 'a farmer without a farm' (p.17). Nugget arrives and invites William to 'help Waxy knock in a few fence posts' (p.18). It seems like a challenge, and one that Nugget knows William will not take up. His parting comment – 'It's called farming, mate' (p.18) – is a subtle hint that William is unfit to inherit the family property.

Scene twelve (pp.18–19)

Summary: *Ashleigh finds an old suitcase containing family memorabilia and a Father Christmas hat and beard.*

Girlie examines the contents of the suitcase and is transported back to the past. She finds '[l]ittle shoes and a curl' belonging to a younger brother, Donald, who 'died of scarlet fever when he was three' (p.18). There is an echo of tragedy here and a reminder that infant mortality was high in the days before modern medicines and vaccinations. The sad relics of a dead child, hidden away for over seventy years, demonstrate that the legacy of the past endures, no matter how deeply buried it is. Girlie's distress at the sight of Ashleigh in the Father Christmas hat and beard suggests another memory from the past, but one that is too painful to confront.

Scene thirteen (pp.19–22)

Summary: *The Berriwillock Road. Nugget arrives to rescue Julia and Felix. Julia and Nugget discuss their respective, failed relationships. Nugget confides in Julia about Farley's plans for the farm.*

Felix is horrified at the racist nickname 'Nugget', and considers it as inappropriate as 'Coon' (p.19). Ironically, Julia, despite her 'Multicultural Commission' credentials, cannot recognise this. Nugget arrives and discusses the breakdown of his relationship, expressing his sympathy for Annie, who was unable to withstand the racist taunts of her students.

As when he experiences other examples of prejudice directed at him (by Lyle, William, and even Dibs and Farley), Nugget is philosophical, perhaps because he recognises the futility of challenging the values of a powerful cultural majority.

Scene fourteen (pp.22–4)

Summary: *Dibs alters a pair of trousers for Farley to wear to the party. Farley's deteriorating mental state and his intolerance of William are again clear. William remembers a childhood visit to the local agricultural show, where Farley refused to allow him to buy a rubber spider.*

Dibs pins up the trousers she has bought at a garage sale, as Farley has refused to buy 'new ones ... for one night': however, he still complains about wearing a 'dead man's trousers' (pp.22–3). He also vents his anger on William, whose sexuality he regards as a 'weakness' (p.23). As Farley becomes increasingly belligerent, Dibs attempts to usher him from the room. She defuses a potentially volatile confrontation between William and Farley, undertaking the traditional maternal responsibility of keeping the peace in the family. While this avoids open conflict, family tensions are driven underground where they remain precariously unreconciled.

Scene fifteen (pp.24–5)

Summary: *At the Delaneys', Lyle and Maureen argue about their finances. Lyle looks through a farm machinery brochure and Maureen angrily reminds him how desperate their financial situation is.*

Maureen is angry at Lyle for looking at farm machinery catalogues when there's no money in the cheque account, but her real anger is directed at Dibs and her 'miserable demented husband' to whom she and Lyle have to pay 'one-third of every dollar [they] earn' (p.25). She tells Brianna to put her pigeons 'in a sack and drown them in the river' because they 'can't afford' to keep them (p.25). Despite her unpleasantness, Maureen evokes a degree of sympathy, as Lyle seems utterly incapable of facing the reality of their deepening financial crisis.

Scene sixteen (pp.25–7)

Summary: *In the Hamiltons' kitchen, William prepares food for the party. Dibs reminisces about her father and his fondness for cream horns. She re-enters the past and relives a scene with her father.*

William's mention of his grandmother's cream horns transports Dibs into the past (p.26). She remembers her father 'trying to scratch a living ... doing every dead-end job he could get' (p.26). Dibs recalls her father's capacity for being the 'life of the party', and also his sudden bouts of depression ('a visit from the black dog', p.27). She confides in William that Norm reminds her of Lyle (p.27): an ominous portent of Lyle's fate. Frequent flashbacks involving Norm reinforce the links between him and Lyle, thus emphasising the inescapability of Lyle's destiny.

Scene seventeen (pp.27–8)

Summary: *Lyle and Brianna enjoy each other's company, laughing and chatting as they cycle into a paddock to release the homing pigeons.*

Temporarily released from domestic and financial pressures, Lyle enjoys his daughter's company. On one level, the conversation he has with her is about training pigeons; on a deeper level it is clearly about farming. He explains: 'You put in the work and you get your rewards. But you gotta have a bit of faith too' (p.27). Ironically, for Lyle and his grandfather, Norm Myrtle, hard work and faith are not sufficient to bring rewards.

Scene eighteen (pp.28–30)

Summary: *In the Delaneys' kitchen, Maureen and Ashleigh have an altercation about the length of Ashleigh's skirt. Girlie speaks to the audience about her experience in Melbourne where, as a young woman, she contracted polio. Lyle and Brianna return and await the arrival of the pigeons.*

Maureen's concern over the length of Ashleigh's skirt reveals her awareness of her daughter's emerging sexuality, and she betrays an implicit adherence to old-fashioned notions about the responsibility of women for controlling men's sexual behaviour. Such conservative values are the basis of Maureen's political ideology. Despite her mother's disapproval, Ashleigh is not willing to look like a 'Salvo' in 'a nice navy' skirt (p.28). Apart from her adolescent fashion-consciousness, Ashleigh's desire to go to Melbourne is driven by a deep resentment of their grinding poverty.

Brianna and Lyle 'charge in on their bikes' just as one of the pigeons arrives, and Norm suddenly 'enters Girlie's memory' (p.29). Girlie recounts the story of one of Norm's prize pigeons that found its way home after having been sold to a Melbourne man (p.30). Brianna asks why Grandpa Norm hanged himself and reveals an intuitive awareness of his (and perhaps Lyle's) desperation and despair: 'Maybe he put in the work and didn't get the rewards' (p.30).

Scene nineteen (pp.30–2)

Summary: *Ashleigh informs Lyle that, according to one of her friends, the Hamiltons are planning to sell the farm. William arrives to borrow trestle tables, and a family argument ensues.*

Lyle and Maureen are angered by Ashleigh's announcement that 'the Hamiltons are going to sell their farm' (p.30), not only because they hear the news second-hand, but also because they will be 'up shit creek' (p.31). In response to Lyle and Maureen's claims that the Delaneys were somehow cheated of their rightful inheritance, William quietly insists that: 'It's [his] family's farm' (p.32). Maureen becomes openly vindictive, calling William 'a pampered city boy who turned tail because he couldn't hack it' (p.32). Family tensions simmer dangerously in this scene, driven by greed, desperation and an unwavering insistence on the perceived rights of inheritance.

Scene twenty (pp.32–5)

Summary: *In the home paddock with Norm and Girlie, looking for water, Young Dibs finds an old coin, which Norm interprets as a sign of good luck. Girlie's future is also 'decided' by the discovery of a coin. On Christmas Day, 1934, Dibs and Girlie find Norm 'swinging from the rafters' in the barn.*

Girlie's sympathetic opening words about Norm echo Maureen's derisive comments about William at the end of the previous scene: 'he just couldn't hack it' (p.32). The inability to 'hack it' is perceived by these characters to be a sign of weakness, as Maureen's criticism of William implies. For Norm, death was perhaps an 'honourable' way out when 'hacking it' became impossible.

In a flashback, Norm finds the 1928 halfpenny – 'the year Bert Hinkler flew solo from the United Kingdom' – and his casual prediction that Dibs will 'marry a very handsome airman' becomes a self-fulfilling prophesy (p.33). Girlie's future, too, is 'determined' by the fall of a coin: Norm tells her she must accept 'how the coin falls and [make] the best of it' (p.33).

Norm gently chastises Girlie for wanting life to be fair and the background Christmas music becomes 'dissonant and unhinged' (p.34), reflecting Norm's growing desperation and despair. The present time re-emerges, with Dibs at the kitchen table. Disconnected fragments from the past enter Girlie's consciousness: a chorus of voices (Norm, Dibs and Girlie) and a 'cacophony of Christmas carols' (p.35). The two young girls push open the barn door, where Norm, 'half-dressed in his Father Christmas suit, is swinging from the rafters' (p.35). Back in the present, eighty-year-old Girlie holds the Father Christmas beard and hat and 'bends down and picks a coin off the ground' (p.35). Again, the merging of past and present is a sombre reminder of the unwanted inheritance of a tragic past.

Scene twenty-one (pp.35–7)

Summary: *Nugget, Julia and Felix arrive at last and are greeted by William, Farley and Dibs. Farley fails to recognise his daughter. Farley and Nugget talk about some nonexistent sheep; William and Julia discuss the future of the farm and the problem of what to do with Farley.*

The arrival of Julia, Felix and Nugget confuses Farley, who asks William if Julia is his 'wife' (p.36), but whether this is genuine bewilderment or another homophobic attack on William is unclear. Farley quickly retreats into a world over which he has some control – talking to his dogs. Alone with Julia on the verandah, William announces his plans to 'rid' his mother of the 'tyrant' she's lived her life with (p.37), suggesting an element of personal revenge in his plans for Farley. Julia has her own agenda. While she is genuinely concerned about Nugget, she is equally concerned about herself now that, as she says later, her 'circumstances have changed' (p.50).

Scene twenty-two (pp.38–9)

Summary: *In the Delaneys' kitchen, Maureen and Lyle discuss the inheritance of the farm and the differences between the Hamiltons and the Delaneys. The issue of Nugget's parentage is also raised, with Girlie speaking her mind about Aboriginal land rights.*

Brianna's sign, 'Banks for People' (p.38) highlights the widespread effects of the rural recession and the ultimate powerlessness of families in the face of the banks' ruthless economic rationalism. Ashleigh's question about 'coons' referring to the land as their 'mother' (p.38) betrays an unconscious racism which is implicitly condoned by her parents, and Maureen launches an attack on Aboriginal land claims (pp.38–9). She also mocks the eagerness of 'university types and do-gooders from the city' (p.38) to expose the injustices of the stolen generations, and Girlie cites Nugget's case, suggesting that all claims about the forcible removal of Aboriginal children are fallacious and perhaps deliberately dishonest (p.39). She concludes with an attack on the 'bloody Mabo mob' (p.39).

Rayson draws a subtle parallel here between dispossessed Aboriginal people and evicted farming families.

Scene twenty-three (pp.39–41)

Summary: *In the Hamiltons' kitchen, Nugget and Felix discuss Felix's university course. Farley insists that Felix dispose of a dead mouse and he and Nugget remember 'Lucky Joe' Delaney. In a rare moment of lucidity, Farley considers his future and admits to being terrified.*

Nugget 'roars laughing' at the description of Felix's university course, 'Cyber Societies' (p.40), which must appear meaningless and self-indulgent to a hard-working, country battler. Nugget's comment: 'that's a killer' is amusingly accompanied by the click of a mousetrap (p.40). Farley's insistence that Felix dispose of the dead mouse displays his utter contempt for his grandson, whom he considers a 'weak little git' (p.40). As Felix unwillingly complies, Nugget and Farley watch him go, united by their disdain of everything he represents.

Nugget's reference to 'Archie Kirkwood' (p.40), as he prepares to cut Farley's hair, triggers a memory which reduces both men to helpless laughter. Nugget's question: 'Can anyone smell burning?' (p.40) is an oblique reference to the 'faggot races', and carries a suggestion that long hair is a sign of effeminacy. Lucky Joe, who 'tipped that whole jug of Vic Bitter ... On Archie's head' (p.41), clearly enjoyed the homophobic ritual as much as Nugget and Farley.

Scene twenty-four (pp.41–3)

Summary: *Lucky Joe and Lofty Blake arrive at a local dance in Rushton in 1937: Joe meets Girlie.*

In another flashback, Girlie fondly remembers meeting Lucky Joe. The scene opens with a reminder of traditional rivalries between Catholics and Protestants (in this case, the Presbyterians). Ironically, Joe's attention is caught by the young Presbyterian 'sheila', Girlie Myrtle, and he wins her heart by refusing to let her disability prevent her from dancing, gallantly asserting that he's 'the envy of every fella in this room' (p.43). In a society where any difference invites discrimination, Joe's disregard of Girlie's disability is unusual.[21] It is ironic therefore that Girlie, whose heart is won by Joe's disregard for her 'difference', becomes so intolerant of differences in others.

Scene twenty-five (pp.43–5)

Summary: *In the Hamiltons' shed, Nugget and Farley set up trestle tables and further reminisce about Lucky Joe. Lyle arrives, drunk and belligerent.*

Nugget distracts both Farley and Lyle (who is threatening to become aggressive) by directing them to set up the trestles and the keg, and Lyle takes the opportunity to raise the issue of the seeder again. Driven by desperation, Lyle turns his anger on Nugget, who refuses to change his mind. Lyle tells Nugget that he's 'just a fuckin' farm hand', and informs him that the farm is being sold so they are 'both up shit creek' (p.44). Clearly unsettled, Nugget dismisses Lyle's revelation as 'bullshit' and takes Farley back to the house, while Lyle mutters: 'Bloody boong … black bastard' (p.44).

According to Lyle, Nugget's Aboriginality renders him incapable of being a farmer: 'they make hopeless bloody farmers' (p.45). Despite his former friendship with Nugget, Lyle endorses the racist attitudes held by many Whites to justify their continued ownership of disputed land.

Scene twenty-six (pp.45–9)

Summary: *Julia, William and Felix walk down the main street of Rushton where Maureen and Girlie are collecting signatures for a petition. Maureen mentions the possible sale of the farm and Girlie slips into the past, remembering the fall of the coin that determined the inheritance of the farm.*

---

[21] In the mid-twentieth century, physical disability was often a source of discrimination; anti-discrimination laws did not protect the rights of disabled people. The *Disability Discrimination Act* was introduced in 1992.

Realising that Girlie and Maureen are up ahead, William wants to '[n]ip down' a side street to avoid them, but it is too late (p.46). Maureen asks 'what's happening about Allandale?' and threatens that 'things might get very nasty' if the farm is sold (p.48). Girlie slips into the past again.

As young Girlie and young Dibs decide to toss for the farm, Girlie reveals that she has not forgiven Norm for '[stringing] himself up' which she describes as 'a sin against God' (p.48). Moreover, Girlie feels that she 'was punished for it. With the polio' (p.48). The question of looking after their mother also arises; it is a duty which goes with the inheritance of the farm. The coin is tossed 'high up into the sky' (p.49) and its fall determines the course of their lives.

Scene twenty-seven (pp.49–57)

Summary: *The Hamilton family, gathered in the dining room for dinner, discuss Maureen's comments about selling the farm.*

The sounds of 'tyres on the gravel and a loud honking' (p.51) herald the arrival of Girlie, who immediately confronts Dibs, demanding 'a decision about the farm [as her] children need to know where they stand' (p.52). Girlie dismisses Farley's claims to Allandale and defiantly asserts her own, claiming that their grandmother, Jessie Allan, 'didn't call it Allandale so some freeloader could just walk in' (p.55). The irony of an argument about the land rights of a white family (which excludes an Aboriginal son) and Nugget's staunch defence of Farley's rights (p.55), is astounding when we reflect on the dispossession of Nugget's ancestors. The tensions between Nugget and Lyle veer dangerously close to physical violence and Nugget 'hauls Lyle outside' so that Maureen can 'take him home' (p.56). An 'ear-piercing scream from Maureen' abruptly ends the discussion as Nugget and Lyle begin fighting (p.57).

Scene twenty-eight (pp.57–8)

Summary: *Nugget and Lyle fight; Lyle shouts racist insults at Nugget; Girlie and Dibs try to stop them. Lyle's hand is damaged by a spade which Nugget slams onto it.*

This is a brief scene, but one which is deeply shocking in the intensity of its physical and verbal violence. The 'vicious and frightening' fight (p.57) and the shouting of obscene and racist insults create a nightmare scenario which engulfs the entire family. Unwilling to hurt his drunken and enraged opponent, Nugget attempts to stop the fight. Finally, he 'shoves' Lyle to the ground and slams down the spade, which catches Lyle's hand as he rolls away. Lyle's agonised scream echoes across the stage as the lights darken to 'Blackout' (p.58).

Act two, scene one (pp.59–61)

Summary: *At the Rushton Show, Maureen Delaney addresses the crowd, which greets her enthusiastically.*

The centrepiece of Maureen's campaign speech is the 'true story' about a 'gang of bikies' threatening to 'trash' the Rushton pub (p.61). Maureen march[ed] over and ordered them out, and they left, obediently and apologetically (p.61). This is intended to illustrate her capacity for standing up for herself and, presumably, for the people of the Mallee. She enjoins her listeners, who 'made this country', not to allow themselves to be 'bullied by foreign interests ... the multinationals' who, she implies, are simply bikies on a larger scale (p.61).

Inexplicably, Maureen switches the focus of her attack from multinational companies to Muslim women 'who are not prepared to show their faces' (p.61), and who are thereby singled out as being particularly un-Australian. If it were not so disturbing, Maureen's rhetoric is almost comically irrational. Designed to appeal to fear and self-interest, it is alarmingly well-received.

Scene two (p.61)

Summary: *Farley's coffin is carried across the stage.*

This brief scene announces the demise of Farley Hamilton and prepares the audience for the final denouement of the long-running 'inheritance' saga.

Scene three (pp.62–9)

Summary: *The family gathers for the funeral; Girlie and Dibs reminisce about Dibs and Farley's wedding. Maureen tells William about Farley's relationship with Nugget's mother. Nugget tells Felix about his mother's death and being taken in by Dibs and Farley.*

Stage directions here highlight family issues, with the older and younger generations separated and Nugget standing alone. Lyle and Maureen arrive later, with Maureen unpinning a 'rosette from her lapel' (p.63). Black humour pervades this scene, beginning with the minister's possible attendance at the wrong cemetery, and irreverent suggestions that Farley 'could have bunked in with the Micks' (p.62). Dibs claims that Farley 'never wanted to be a farmer' and Girlie responds that they were all 'trapped into doing things [they] didn't want to do' (p.63).

Key point

Entrapment, Girlie implies, is an inescapable part of inheritance: we are unable to choose what we inherit (in either a material or biological sense) and are bound by an imperative to pass on a tradition. There is more than a hint of bitterness in Girlie's comment.

In a 'private aside with William', Maureen suggests that he and Julia should 'move quickly' if they want 'a piece of the action' (p.65). It is a crass and highly inappropriate comment, but she ignores the reproof from Julia and refers, indelicately, to 'the other business' (p.65). William is horrified by the nature and timing of Maureen's claims that Farley 'took advantage' of Nugget's mother (p.66). William is uncharacteristically defensive, describing Farley as 'a man of rigid morality' and Maureen as a 'poisonous witch' (p.66). With a parting shot – 'Your father porked a gin' – Maureen leaves.

The minister arrives and the men lift the coffin. The family exits, 'leaving behind Nugget and Felix' (p.67). Nugget explains that he and Farley were 'real mates' (p.67) and that Dibs and Farley took him in because 'they're the most Christian people you're ever likely to meet' (p.69). Again, as is so often the case, the scene resonates with irony.

Scene four (pp.69–72)

Summary: *Julia and Dibs sort through Farley's wardrobe and discuss family matters: Hamish's sexuality, Nugget's parentage and Julia's pregnancy. They argue about the farm. Julia tells Dibs about William's problems in his relationship with Kevin.*

Dibs expresses her disappointment that Julia didn't 'try hard enough' (p.69) with Hamish, despite the fact that he is homosexual. Dibs betrays her lack of understanding of homosexuality, assuming it can be 'cured' by a woman. She also betrays her racism, implying that Julia's boyfriend is not 'a proper man' because he is Indian (p.70). Julia's desire to return to a simple life in the country is in direct opposition to William's needs, which involve selling the farm to help finance his plans for a vineyard on the Mornington Peninsula, and consolidating his relationship with Kevin. Dibs quietly savours the power she holds over both her children by avoiding a resolution of the question of their inheritance.

Scene five (pp.72–3)

Summary: *Girlie informs Maureen that the bank has served them with an eviction notice. She blames Nugget, who allegedly went back on a promise to contribute half the cost of the seeder.*

Lyle's irritability as he listens to the races suggests that he has bet on a horse in a desperate attempt to avoid foreclosure by the bank. Girlie's announcement that they've had 'a visit from the bailiff' (p.73), and that Lyle has put the house up as security on a loan, evokes a furious outburst from Maureen. She screams at Lyle, calling him a 'hopeless bloody loser' (p.73). Lyle has apparently told Girlie that Nugget let him down by backing out of an agreement, but it is clear that Lyle is unable to face the consequences of his financial recklessness.

Scene six (pp.74–7)

Summary: *William and Dibs find Farley's will, which names Nugget as the heir to the estate, and Dibs tears it up. Nugget enters, looking for the will, and realises that he's been cheated of his inheritance.*

William and Dibs collude to deprive Nugget of his rightful inheritance by tearing up Farley's will. Their actions are not only illegal, they are unconscionable – driven by self-interest, spite and racism. Nugget arrives to discover that there is 'nothing in here' for him (p.77) despite Farley's promise to leave him the farm (p.76). Dibs wants to keep Allandale 'in the family' (p.77), but Dibs and William's unwillingness to admit that Nugget belongs in the family ultimately costs them the farm.

Scene seven (pp.77–9)

Summary: *Felix and Julia discuss Farley's relationship with Nugget's mother. William enters; he still refuses to believe that Farley was Nugget's father.*

The historical fact of Aboriginal women's exploitation by white men is raised by Julia, who is disgusted at her father's behaviour, while Felix is disgusted by the thought of anyone wanting to have sex with his grandfather (p.77). Julia takes a feminist perspective and even feels sympathy for her mother, while Felix again reveals his prejudice about age – as he did when he declared that Julia (at forty-four) was 'a bit old' to have a baby (p.13).

William reiterates his belief that Farley 'did not touch that girl' and insists that Julia and Felix are not to indulge in 'some leftie guilt trip' (p.78). As Julia, William and Felix insult each other, Julia observes that

William sounds 'just like Dad' (p.79). William says grace, and the sound of the choir intrudes once more with 'Praise My Soul, the King of Heaven' (p.79), providing a further example of an ironic disjunction between Christian sentiments and un-Christian behaviour.

Scene eight (pp.79–80)

Summary: *The Delaneys (who have been evicted) arrive on the Hamiltons' doorstep with all their possessions.*

The opening of this very brief scene provides strong visual evidence of the Delaneys' desperate plight, and Lyle's 'offer' of help to Dibs (p.80) is a futile attempt to disguise his loss of dignity. The continued singing of the choir implies that 'praising' God has provided little comfort to families like the Delaneys. Father Kelly, the local representative of the Catholic Church, has been reduced to an ineffectual figure, capable only of whistling 'Ramona' at the annual concert (p.72).

Scene nine (pp.80–1)

Summary: *The arrival of the Delaneys evokes outrage from William and the aura of general chaos is intensified. Evidence of the mouse plague is comically emphasised when a mouse runs up Felix's trousers.*

William reveals himself to be completely heartless, referring to the Delaneys as 'parasites' (p.81). He is also thinking about his claim on the farm, accusing Girlie of 'trying to take over [the] estate' (pp.80–1). Suddenly, the mood becomes almost farcical as a mouse runs up Felix's trousers: he screams then 'reaches inside his trouser leg and throws out a mouse' which Dibs 'stomps on' (p.81). No-one escapes Rayson's critical eye in this play – the flaws, foibles and darkest secrets of all the characters are clearly exposed, in ways that are sometimes humorous but always confronting.

Scene ten (p.82)

Summary: *Ashleigh bitterly resents Lyle for plunging the family into debt and verbally attacks him.*

Although she is her mother's daughter, Ashleigh Delaney is also an adolescent facing a crisis which engulfs her. Her friends, such as Teaghan Kelly, seem to have normal lives and Ashleigh is overwhelmed by the humiliation of being different. This also partly explains (but does not excuse) her homophobic attack on William. Just as Rayson exposes the darker side of those we might wish to sympathise with, she provides glimmers of insight into characters like Maureen and Ashleigh. It is the multi-layered quality of her characters that makes Rayson's plays so 'real' and interesting.

Key point

Ashleigh's bitter statement, 'you don't borrow money when you're like up to your eyeballs in debt' (p.82) recognises Lyle's foolishness, but it is also a powerful indictment of the bank for its moral irresponsibility in approving loans to those who cannot repay them.

Scene eleven (pp.82–5)

Summary: *The props in this scene show the impact of the mouse plague and the inadequacy of farmers' attempts to control the forces of nature. Julia and Lyle discuss the recent hostility between Nugget and Lyle; Maureen, Julia and Felix argue and insult each other.*

Lyle tries to explain to Felix and Julia why he and Nugget are no longer 'mates', but this is immediately construed by Felix as racism (p.83). Lyle is angry because Felix is right, but he dismisses Felix's views as those of a 'city boy' who doesn't know what it's like having to 'live with them' (p.83). Lyle's racist comment demonstrates a resentful attitude towards city people, whom he sees as judgemental and as having little knowledge of his life in the country. Lyle's judgements are based on his own flawed perceptions and financial problems. Maureen's arrival provokes further heated discussion, with Felix accusing Maureen of campaigning against Nugget's appointment to a local government position (p.84). Her self-righteous response is very evocative of Pauline Hanson's One Nation rhetoric.

Scene twelve (pp.85–6)

Summary: *Overcome by guilt, Dibs sobs and confesses to Girlie that she tore up Farley's will. Girlie approves, and suggests they treat themselves to a weekend away. Dibs admits that she knows Nugget is Farley's son.*

Dibs' deep remorse, and her concern over Nugget's future, temporarily redeem her; however, she reveals herself to be bitter and vindictive, justifying her actions because Farley has handed over her 'family farm to his bastard son' (p.86). Dibs vehemently asserts that Nugget is not going to get 'a single handful of this dirt' (p.86), demonstrating that her resentment of Farley is stronger than either her morality or her affection for Nugget.

Scene thirteen (pp.87–8)

Summary: *Farley speaks from beyond the grave, acknowledging his affection and paternal responsibility for Nugget. This does not extend, however, to acknowledging his paternity, and it is because of his failure to do so that Nugget is disinherited.*

Nugget recalls Farley telling him that he was 'no different to anyone else in this family', and Farley states that he 'never thought of [Nugget] as a blackfella' (p.87), yet he denies his paternity by refusing to 'speak the truth'. Farley also denies Nugget an opportunity to claim his Aboriginal 'inheritance'. Nugget remembers seeing Aboriginal people in Swan Hill, who would smile but think: 'he's with them now' (p.87). Nugget has been denied his rightful inheritance on two counts: ownership of his land and connection with his Aboriginal culture and family. Farley's justification – 'Some things are best left unsaid' (p.88) – sounds exceedingly hollow.

Scene fourteen (pp.88–9)

Summary: *Lyle is again drunk; he drives into a paddock at night, shouting, swearing, drinking and firing a gun into the air.*

Lyle's 'expensive, powerful car stereo' is another indication of his financial mismanagement. As 'a farmer without a farm' (p.89), he no longer sees a purpose in life. In a drunken orgy of self-pity, Lyle admits the folly of having a 'big header, big car, big ideas, big mortgage' (pp.88–9), dimly recognising the dreadful cost of trying to prove his worth in the traditionally 'masculine' ways expected by a patriarchal society.

Scene fifteen (pp.89–90)

Summary: *Dibs and Girlie sip chardonnay, seated at a table in the Grand Hotel in Mildura. Girlie admits to never having liked William very much.*

Released from the tensions of family squabbles, Dibs and Girlie enjoy each other's company. Dibs confides in Girlie that she dislikes William: 'He always acts like I owe him. Because he had such a hard time with Farley' (p.90). Girlie claims that Felix is 'a bloody wuss' (p.90), for which Dibs blames his vegan diet. While Felix's rather extreme dietary regime is no doubt incomprehensible to these practical country women, Dibs and Girlie's self-assurance verges on arrogance. Girlie's humorous (and perhaps deliberate) incomprehension of the word 'vegan' suggests that Felix's differences render him alien in the eyes of his conservative country relatives.

Scene sixteen (pp.90–3)

Summary: *In the Hamiltons' woolshed, Felix is smoking pot; Brianna enters, looking for Ashleigh. She becomes distressed and Felix comforts her. Drunk and irrational, Lyle enters and misconstrues Felix's sympathetic hug of Brianna as a sexual advance; he whips Felix viciously and repeatedly across the face.*

Felix and Brianna discuss the inheritance of the farm, each arguing on the grounds of 'spiritual attachment': Nugget's and Lyle's. This is the crux of the debate, and pinpoints the issues that make it irresolvable. Becoming distressed, Brianna tells Felix about Lyle's pigeon, 'Little Red', which Lyle believes did not return because 'a beautiful bird' would not 'waste her time hanging out with [him]' (p.91).

As Felix puts his arms around her, Lyle flings open the door and 'strides towards Felix, shaking with drunken rage' (p.91). The vicious beating he inflicts on Felix is the final straw for Maureen, who tells him to leave and not to come back. Felix is badly injured and traumatised, while Lyle remains highly volatile and dangerous as he 'slinks away into the night' (p.92).

Scene seventeen (p.93)

Summary: *Dibs and Girlie continue to enjoy themselves in Mildura, blissfully unaware of the dreadful events at Allandale. Girlie embarks on a subtle campaign to convince Dibs to leave the farm to Lyle.*

Another brief scene, cutting away from dramatic events at Allandale, draws out the tension of Lyle's frenzied demise. Girlie soothes and gently flatters her sister, telling her what a 'good job' she's done with her children, and how much Lyle 'loves his Aunty Dibs'.

Scene eighteen (pp.93–5)

Summary: *Felix has not spoken since the night in the woolshed and has needed fourteen stitches in his face. Ashleigh rushes in with the story about Lyle driving the tractor through the bank's plate glass window.*

The less he has left to lose, the more reckless Lyle becomes. His self-respect has vanished, his marriage is over, his house has been repossessed and even his favourite pigeon has deserted him. Lyle's public act of mindless vandalism is a final futile gesture of defiance. The irrational anger unleashed in the paddock is now directed against the bank: a symbol of all the external forces that have combined to destroy him.

Scene nineteen (p.95)

Summary: *Dibs legally transfers the property to Lyle.*

The sisters' pleasure in their decision and optimism for the future contrast poignantly with the fragmentation of their families. Dibs' confident assertion that she's 'kept [the farm] in the family' proves to be highly ironic in the light of Maureen's later disposal of her inheritance, while the role of the law in Nugget's dispossession is a grim echo of colonial land acquisitions.

Scene twenty (p.96)

Summary: *Ashleigh and Brianna, dressed in their blue school uniforms, discover Lyle swinging from the rafters; brimming with excitement, Dibs and Girlie head back to Allandale, singing 'Two Little Girls in Blue'.*

Lyle fulfils his tragic destiny, following in the footsteps of his grandfather as his genetic inheritance is ironically juxtaposed with his inheritance of Allandale.

Epilogue (pp.97–8)

Summary: *Maureen is poised to win the seat of Murray as a new independent member of parliament. Julia, Nugget and Felix watch the telecast of an interview with Maureen.*

Heady with victory, Maureen declares that selling the farm will 'save [the] country' (p.97). Her belief that she can accomplish this is a measure of her arrogance, but also of her naivety. Nugget asks Felix to turn the television off and the lights darken to blackout – as they did at the end of Act one after the fight between Nugget and Lyle. The blackout here is similarly gloomy, implying that the politics of racism will usher in a dark era in Australian history.

CHARACTERS & RELATIONSHIPS

Norm Myrtle

Key quotes

He'd be laughing away ... and then he'd get a visit from the black dog.' (Dibs: p.27)

'That's the hardest lesson in life ... Accepting how the coin falls and making the best of it.' (p.33)

'If I could just stop thinking. Stop this scratching inside my skull.' (p.34)

'Whoever said life was fair? Life is not fair.' (p.34)

Significance of name

Myrtle is a symbolic plant for the Jews, being one of four plants used in the Sukkoth festival, which celebrates the harvest and commemorates the period during which the Jews wandered in the wilderness after the Exodus. The family name may have some significance in connection with the idea of exile in the wilderness, and the need to transform a place of exile into one of belonging by establishing a permanent presence in the landscape. 'Myrtle' (the flower, and a name once often given to girls) also has feminine connotations, implying perhaps that there is some stereotypically 'masculine' attribute lacking in Norm – indeed, his inability to produce a living male heir might support such a reading. Nevertheless, in a play that questions the appropriateness of gender stereotypes, this is not a condemnation of Norm.

Character & relationships

Patriarch, life of the party, depressive personality, home and family of utmost importance.

Home and family are sacred to Norm. His beloved pigeons symbolise the importance of home through their uncanny ability to return home across vast distances. Norm's strong connection with the natural world is also evident in his gift for 'water divining' (p.32), and if a 'spiritual attachment' (p.91) implies rights of ownership then Norm seems to qualify, although his claims lack the historical validity of Nugget's. Norm struggles to make ends meet: 'Trapping rabbits. Chopping wood. Filling in at the butchers' (p.26). Yet he can find humour in adversity and the 'chicken enhancing' episode (pp.26–7) demonstrates his resilience and resourcefulness. These qualities do not save him, however, from a tragic death.

Crisis point

Norm could be the 'life of the party' but often he'd 'get a visit from the black dog' (p.27).[22] Norm's suicide, which leaves him suspended from the rafters 'half-dressed in his Father Christmas suit' (p.35), rather grotesquely highlights the comic and tragic sides of his personality.

Dibs Hamilton

Key quotes

'I love being down in Melbourne ... It's everything I've always dreamed of.' (p.48)

'I never wanted the farm.' (p.57)

'I stood by him [Farley] all that time – and then he goes and does this.' (p.86)

'He [William] always acts like I owe him. Because he had such a hard time with Farley.' (p.90)

'Here's to us. Eighty years old and still going strong.' (p.93)

Character & relationships

Conservative, resilient, loyal, dutiful, controlling, bitter, vindictive.

Dibs' life has been shaped by acceptance of her fate and a strong sense of duty. The chance discovery and toss of a coin leads Dibs 'to marry a very handsome airman' (p.33) and to inherit Allandale. She takes her duty

---

[22] A number of people who have firsthand experience of depression have described their depression as a 'black dog' – famous among them was British Prime Minister Winston Churchill, who used the term 'black dog' to describe the crippling depression he suffered throughout his lifetime. It is thought that the term has even earlier origins.

seriously, giving up dreams of nursing in Melbourne (p.48). William's promise of a 'brand new home' with 'No possums pissing in the roof' (p.17) sounds attractive, yet her awareness of how 'truly awful' it would be for Farley to leave the farm (p.16), and the fact that Nugget would be 'a farmer without a farm' (p.17), hold her back. Dibs dutifully fulfils the role of the loyal wife, supporting Farley's rights to ownership of Allandale (p.55).

However, Dibs knows 'Farley's secret' (p.86), although she has never discussed Nugget's paternity with Farley or with anyone else. After Farley dies, Dibs loyally insists that he was 'a good man' and that no-one should 'sling mud at him' (p.72). Yet a deep bitterness surfaces as she wonders: 'What sort of a man' would 'hand over [her] family farm to his bastard son' (p.86). Despite the fact that she 'raised Nugget [and] she loves him' (p.84), Dibs vindictively refuses to 'honour [Farley's] dying wishes' (p.86) and acknowledge Nugget as his heir.

Dibs' relationships with her children seem harmonious. Yet she finally admits that if she told 'the God-honest truth – [she doesn't] really like [William] that much' (p.90). She confides in the audience about her 'disappointment' over the failure of Julia's marriage, admitting that she 'misses' Julia's ex-husband, Hamish, and implying that Julia is 'selfish' (p.5). Dibs' condemnation of 'young women' (such as Julia) indicates her unquestioning endorsement of a traditional maternal and domestic role as the proper one for women (p.5). Perhaps Dibs' most meaningful relationship is with her sister. This becomes strained as their families battle over who will inherit the property. Despite the differences in their fortunes and their disagreements – even over small issues like fertilising the roses (p.5) – Dibs often seems closer to her sister than to her husband or her children, perhaps because of a shared genetic inheritance.

Crisis point

Dibs' crises involve moral decisions about Nugget's future. Although she feels betrayed by Farley's infidelity, Dibs sees it as her Christian duty to offer his 'bastard son' a home, as Joyce's family 'couldn't look after him like [she and Farley] could' (p.86). The discovery of Farley's altered will, favouring Nugget, is a potential crisis, quickly resolved by tearing it up (p.75). Nugget's adoption and disinheritance reflect crisis points in white Australia's relations with Aboriginal Australia: the stolen generations and issues regarding land rights. Just as Dibs punishes Farley, she too is punished by being disinherited – ironically by the very measures she has taken to keep the farm 'in the family' (p.95).

Farley Hamilton

Key quotes

'I'm just a miserable old skinflint.' (p.23)

'If you're going to waste my hard-earned money on rubbish, I'll take it back.' (Farley, recalled by William: p.24)

'Don't let them take me. I'm going mad.' (p.41)

'Some things are best left unsaid, mate.' (p.88)

Character & relationships

Intolerant, prejudiced, bad-tempered, miserly, bitter, vulnerable, afraid.

Farley is a stubborn, irascible and unpleasant old man, who makes no attempt to conceal his homophobia. When William arrives, Farley barely acknowledges his son's presence (pp.10–11). His bitterness is driven by his belief that William made no effort to 'overcome' his 'weakness' (p.23). Farley's relationship with Nugget, on the other hand, is a loving and mutually supportive one. Farley teaches Nugget how to 'kick the footy' (p.67), and as Farley deteriorates mentally, Nugget gently reassures him that he's 'lookin' out for [him]' (p.41). Farley 'squeezes Nugget's hand even tighter' (p.41), demonstrating his affection for his 'adopted' son. He finally recognises Nugget as his legitimate son by leaving him the farm, but Nugget is disinherited by Dibs because of Farley's inability to 'tell them the truth' (p.88).

Farley is also 'a miserable old skinflint' who complains that buying new trousers for one night is 'bloody ridiculous' (p.23). He is bitter about the years spent 'scrimping' so he could send his son to Scotch College,[23]

[23] Scotch College, Melbourne, is an elite private boys school.

and begrudges 'frittering away all that money. On education' without ever producing any results (p.23). Farley exemplifies the complexity of Rayson's characters: for all his disagreeable, prickly irritability, he is also a pathetic, ageing man who 'never wanted to be a farmer' (p.63).

Crisis point

Faced with his inability to remember, Farley is suddenly 'gripped by a moment of terror'. He 'grasps Nugget's hand', pleading: 'Don't let them take me. I'm going mad' (p.41).

William Hamilton

Key quotes

'It's my family's farm.' (p.32)

'A stud with a guilty secret.' (p.46)

'Our father did not touch that girl.' (p.78)

'These people [the Delaneys] are parasites.' (p.81)

Character & relationships

Victim of prejudice, witty, eloquent and sophisticated, self-centred, calculating, lacking in compassion.

The homophobic prejudice of his rural community, with its ritual 'faggot races' (p.8), and his father's overt hostility, invite our sympathy for William. Defensively perhaps, William develops an acerbic wit: he calls his father 'Der Führer' (p.10) and accuses him of being 'operatic' (p.11). While his relationship with Dibs appears to be harmonious (p.9), William is not surprised by his mother's deeply ingrained prejudice, 'shak[ing] his head' resignedly at her comment that 'nobody need know' that Kevin is gay (p.10).

As the play unfolds, however, William reveals himself to be self-seeking, arrogant and ruthless. While the family bickers about who should inherit Allandale, Nugget's defence of Farley evokes a deliberately humiliating reproof from William, who coldly informs Nugget that this 'is a matter for family' (p.55). William's solicitous concern for his mother's welfare is rightly construed by Julia as self-interest: as she says to Dibs, 'William wants you to sell this place because he's scared of losing Kevin' (p.72). And while Julia is also motivated by self-interest, she is not callous. William's reference to the homeless and destitute Delaneys as 'parasites' reveals his utter incapacity for 'human charity' (p.81). Ironically, William becomes as self-righteous and intolerant as his father was, and even begins to 'sound just like' him (p.79).

Nugget Hamilton

Key quotes

'They'd be up shit creek, you know, if it wasn't for me.' (p.21)

'See, me and Farley, we've always had an understanding.' (p.22)

'This is my country. This should be my farm. But they've pulled the fucking rug from under me.' (p.87)

'... you wouldn't tell them the truth.' (p.88)

Character & relationships

Loyal, hard-working, trusting, reliable, sensible, frustrated, exploited.

Nugget represents both his dispossessed Aboriginal ancestors and those members of the stolen generations who were assimilated into well-meaning Christian families in order to have 'a proper home ... and proper schooling' (p.86); for this, he (like his ancestors) is expected to be 'grateful' (p.76). However, Nugget's education is at Longerenong Agricultural College (p.45), whereas William's is at Scotch College.

Given his second-rung status in the family, Nugget is (rightly) concerned that Dibs will leave him 'high and dry' (p.21). He knows that he is 'Farley's son' (p.76), and that carving the farm up would make it unprofitable. Furthermore, he is very aware of his ancestral rights as an Aboriginal person, as is clearly implied by his assertion that: 'This is my country. This should be my farm' (p.87). On economic, moral and historical grounds, his claims are shown to be entirely valid, but they are undermined by family greed and prejudice.

Key point

Nugget himself is not entirely free from prejudice, preferring not 'to think about' William's relationship with Kevin (p.20). Despite this, Nugget is perhaps the moral centre of the play; he is loyal, honest, reliable and unselfish and bears no ill will those who have wronged him.

Crisis point

After Farley's death, Nugget realises that he has been dispossessed by 'an exclusionary white world'.[24] The fact that Farley 'always treated [him] like a son' (p.87) does not safeguard his rights.

Julia Hamilton

Key quotes

'I am not the little girl who comes home from boarding school anymore.' (p.50)

'I wanted a man as well as a baby, actually.' (p.70)

'I'm stressed out of my brain ... I want to change my life.' (p.71)

'I've never hated anyone as much as I hate that animal [Lyle] and if I saw him now I'd go at him with a knife.' (p.94)

Character & relationships

Impulsive, generous, vulnerable, unsettled, sympathetic, outspoken.

Julia endeavours to bridge the cultural divide between country and city. Born in Rushton but educated in Melbourne, she (unlike William) 'love[s] coming up' to Allandale (p.37). She retains quaint aspects of a rough rural inheritance, remembering the annual 'faggot races' as 'pretty funny' (p.8). Julia consciously rejects a stereotypical version of femininity – as her completing a course in 'Car Maintenance For Women' (p.4) indicates.

[24] Hilary Glow, 'Speaking truth to power: Hannie Rayson's '*Inheritance*'', in Hannie Rayson, *Inheritance*, p.x.

She also pursues a career in the Multicultural Commission; however, Julia is unsettled. Numerous failed enterprises reveal that she is not good at 'seeing things through' (p.50). Her desire for 'a man as well as a baby' (p.70) suggests a desire for fulfilment which is connected with a return to more traditional notions of the feminine. She enters into problematic relationships: following her marriage with Hamish (who is gay), she has a relationship with Graham, and possibly also with Amitav – Indian colleagues at the Multicultural Commission.

Julia is a complex character, caught between conflicting values and loyalties, and while this is unsettling, there is a sense in which she is open to new possibilities. The impending birth of her child, whose parents represent the old colonial establishment and the new multicultural Australia, suggests possibilities for achieving a balance between the opposing forces that divide Australians in the twenty-first century – a divide that Maureen Delaney seeks actively to reinforce.

Crisis point

Lyle's vicious beating of Felix (p.92) unleashes bitter hatred in Julia. She is also abruptly awakened to the stark reality of the idyllic country life she craves – a part of the 'unspoiled charm' of rural Australia is its lack of medical services (p.93).

Felix Hamilton-Gray

Key quotes

'I still can't believe we call him Nugget.' (p.19)

'She's a Christian. They do all sorts of weird shit.' (p.67)

'I think I might head back tomorrow, Mum. Now the asylum seekers have moved in.' (p.84)

'Jesus Christ. Help me.' (p.93)

Character & relationships

Condescending, cynical, sympathetic, self-assured, vulnerable.

Felix is a 'city boy' (p.83) whose cynicism is his buffer against the vulnerability of his youth and his non-stereotypical masculinity. The play certainly raises questions (articulated by Maureen and Girlie) about Felix's sexuality: 'He's a weedy-looking bloke ... He does look like a fairy' (p.46). The point is, however, not whether Felix is gay, but rather how men are judged when they do not conform to 'acceptable' ways of being masculine. Unable to participate in traditional displays of brute strength or sporting ability, Felix, like his uncle William, develops verbal dexterity and a capacity for cynical humour. This is often deliberately cutting: his reference to the homeless Delaneys as 'asylum seekers', for example, confronts Maureen with an uncomfortable parallel between her family and stateless political refugees (p.84).

Like all the other characters in the play, Felix is not untainted by prejudice: asked by Dibs to 'say grace', Felix's 'horrified' reaction reveals deeply anti-Christian sentiments (p.51). He is quick, however, to take the moral high ground when others reveal their prejudices and he is incapable of being 'pleasant' to Maureen because of her 'obnoxious' politics (p.84). Nevertheless, Felix's understanding of Nugget's 'spiritual attachment' to the land, and his sympathy for Brianna (p.91), reveal a capacity for compassion which goes beyond the mere display of what is 'politically correct' (p.85).

Crisis point

Lyle's savage beating leaves Felix in a state of shock. This is a brutal awakening for Felix to the harsh realities of a chaotic adult world, which his course in 'Cyber Societies' (p.39) has not prepared him for. At the height of Felix's crisis, there is a rather grimly amusing irony in his evocation of the name of 'Jesus Christ' (p.93).

Girlie Delaney

Key quotes

'They're thieves, those Greeks!' (p.15)

'It's bad luck, that place [Melbourne].' (p.29)

'I want to marry an airman. It's not fair.' (Young Girlie: p.34)

'One of us takes on the farm and the other is free to go.' (Young Girlie: p.48)

'... this farm does not belong to Farley. He's made a damn good living out of it. But it is not his land.' (p.55)

Character & relationships

Stubborn, proud, loyal, resilient, tenacious, prejudiced, bitter, scheming.

Girlie initially seems to be an admirably feisty old lady as she 'hoons across the stage' on her motorised lawnmower (p.8). She loyally defends Lyle, believing that he is cursed by bad luck rather than guilty of bad management. Girlie had a loving relationship with Lucky Joe and a close relationship with Norm, cemented by their love of pigeons, despite the fact that he sentences her to a life of 'duty' (p.33). However, she blames him for her polio, claiming that she was 'punished' for his 'sin against God' in '[stringing] himself up' (p.48). Perhaps because of her hard life, Girlie is tough and resilient, speaking her mind in no uncertain terms. Initially, her prejudice is so wide-ranging, so completely outrageous, that it is a source of humour: she attacks migrants, homosexuals, vegetarians and even Presbyterians. In this respect, Rayson's portrayal of Girlie veers very close to caricature.

As the narrative unfolds, however, Girlie is revealed as a querulous old woman with a chip on her shoulder. She is bitter over the Hamiltons' inheritance of the farm and becomes increasingly driven by her need for Lyle to inherit Allandale. She is fiercely proud of her descent from Jessie Allan and sees Lyle as Allandale's natural heir, as he 'was born just on harvest', a portentous sign of 'a good farmer' (p.93). Girlie's invitation to her sister to spend a weekend at the Grand Hotel in Mildura might be viewed as a cynical attempt to ensure Lyle's succession by convincing Dibs to give him 'a leg up' (p.93). This backfires dramatically when Maureen inherits and sells the property.

Lyle Delaney

Key quotes

'You can't wait for things to come to you ... You've got to make things happen.' (p.12)

'You put in the work and you get your rewards. But you gotta have a bit of faith too.' (p.27)

'Who says life is fair? Life is not fair.' (p.31)

'I love this place.' (p.89)

'Why would a beautiful bird like Little Red waste her time hanging out with me?' (recalled by Brianna: p.91)

Character & relationships

Stubborn, passionate, loving, ambitious, independent, moody, violent, unreasonable, desperate, tragic.

Lyle's genetic 'inheritance' from his grandfather largely determines his fate. Like his grandfather, he is moody and passionate and he has a love of pigeons. Increasingly oppressed by debt, Lyle enjoys a temporary respite as he and Brianna release the pigeons to 'make the most' of their freedom (p.28). We sense Lyle's own need for freedom, and have a glimpse of what he might be like if his circumstances were different. Lyle is also a loving son, proudly presenting his mother with a motorised lawnmower, which will 'make all the difference to [her] life' (p.6). Driven by his need to be his 'own boss', Lyle tries to talk Nugget into putting in 'fifty grand' and going 'halves' in a seeder (p.12). However, Nugget resists, realising that Lyle is 'in over [his] neck' (p.44).

As he becomes more desperate, Lyle drinks heavily and becomes bitterly resentful of Nugget. He goads and humiliates Nugget, calling him a 'fucking shit-arsed coon' and accusing him of being 'pissweak' (pp.57–8). Lyle foolishly borrows the money – convincing himself that Nugget will relent – and then claims that Nugget has 'backed out' of the deal (p.73). When the bank finally serves an eviction notice and Maureen and Ashleigh turn on him with bitter recriminations, Lyle drives the tractor down the main street and through the bank's plate glass window (p.94). In a drunken rage, he savagely attacks Felix, who is trying to comfort Brianna and Maureen orders him to leave – and not to come back (p.93). As his mother and aunt arrange for Lyle to inherit Allandale, Lyle embraces the tragic fate of his grandfather and hangs himself from the rafters in the barn.

Key point

If *Inheritance* is a tragedy, then Lyle is its tragic hero – cursed with a 'fatal flaw' and battling against external forces beyond his control.

Crisis point

Lyle reaches crisis point as his personal failings and external forces combine to crush him. He loses faith in himself and traditional support structures such as religion, community and family. Lyle turns to the bank – which seems to offer a way out – and finally to alcohol. In the end, death is the only escape.

Maureen Delaney

Key quotes

'It's bloody feudal. We're living like peasants.' (p.25)

'... things might get very nasty around here.' (p.48)

'... you two better move quickly. If you want a piece of the action.' (p.65)

'There is nothing racist about my policies.' (p.84)

'You're so politically correct, you wouldn't know your arse from your armpit.' (p.85)

Character & relationships

Outspoken, prejudiced, assertive, opportunistic, confident, harsh, tunnel-visioned, frustrated.

Along with her mother-in-law, Girlie, Maureen Delaney is the repository of much of the prejudice in the play. She is racist, homophobic and xenophobic, yet we cannot simply dismiss her as evil. She is a simple-minded woman who sees the world in black-and-white terms and she firmly believes that she can solve the country's economic problems with her 'common-sense' approach. On the basis of her own limited experience, Maureen constructs a political ideology that strikes a chord with other disaffected country dwellers who, like her, feel betrayed by the government. Energised by her frustration, Maureen is not prepared to sit back and do nothing while her husband drinks, gambles and plunges the family deeper into debt.

Yet Maureen's willingness to blame 'every Asian, Moslem and Hottentot who come here and refuse to sign up to the Australian Way of Life' cannot be condoned (p.61). She plays to the xenophobia of those who blame 'outsiders' for the country's social and economic problems. She becomes increasingly harsh and bitter, calling Lyle a 'hopeless piece of trash' and a 'useless idiot' (p.73). William's description of Maureen as a 'poisonous witch' seems justified as she takes the opportunity at Farley's funeral to inform his family that Farley 'porked a gin' (p.66). That Maureen sells the farm to finance her political campaign shows a brutal disregard for the family, who have struggled to preserve their inheritance for 'five generations' (p.97). However, the family's ownership of the farm raised significant moral dilemmas, and a kind of rough moral justice – with Maureen as its agent – is served by its loss.

Crisis point

Maureen's crisis is precipitated by the combination of Lyle's financial mismanagement and the rural recession. Like Lyle, Maureen blames the wrong people, but unlike Lyle, she turns misfortune around and (aided by a stroke of luck) emerges as a survivor.

Lucky Joe Delaney

Key quotes

'He was such a funny man. You know you're blessed if you've found a bloke who can make you laugh.' (Girlie: p.41)

'Can't walk don't mean you can't dance.' (p.42)

'I'm the envy of every fella in this room.' (p.43)

Character & relationships

Joe Delaney is the stereotypical, larrikin 'Aussie'. Descended, in all probability, from convict stock, he made his own luck, capitalised on his skills and charmed his way into the establishment. Along with the athleticism he displayed in winning the Stawell Gift, and his shrewdness in making 'eight hundred quid' by backing himself to win (p.43), Joe was a smooth talker who won Girlie's heart with his easy charm, persuading crippled Girlie to dance by claiming that she 'won't show [him] up' (p.42). Although he, too, is tainted by his religious prejudice, this does not stop him marrying one of 'those Presbyterian sheilas' (p.42). Such is Joe's charisma that even Farley, who considers 'Micks' (Catholics) to be 'peasants' and 'bloody bog Irish' (pp.43–4), thinks fondly of Joe as one of 'the good ones' (p.41).

Ashleigh Delaney

Key quotes

'I hate that skirt. I look like a Salvo.' (p.28)

'What do coons mean when they say the land is 'my mother'?' (p.38)

'Even a baby knows you don't borrow money when you're like up to your eyeballs in debt.' (p.82)

Character & relationships

Ashleigh is self-centred, shallow and, like her mother and grandmother, highly prejudiced. She is humiliated by her family's financial problems and bitterly unforgiving of her father. She resents having to move in with a 'poofter' and regards her father as a 'fucking loser' (p.82). Ashleigh inherits her mother's attitudes, and shows how prejudice is perpetuated through generations, as children often unthinkingly adopt their parents' values.

Brianna Delaney

Key quotes

'Yous are so racist.' (p.38)

'We belong here too.' (p.91)

Character & relationships

Brianna has a loving relationship with Lyle, with whom she shares a passion for pigeons, and is sympathetic to his plight. She believes that 'it's not his fault' and that 'whatever decision [he] makes, it doesn't work out' (p.91). This reveals Brianna's love for her father. It also shows her understanding that there are powerful external forces operating against Lyle and that he is fulfilling a tragic destiny. It is Brianna who intuitively understands Lyle's connection with his grandfather Norm, who also 'put in the work and didn't get the rewards' (p.30). She is appalled at her sister's racist comments and has clearly not adopted her parents' values.

THEMES, IDEAS & VALUES

Inheritance

Key quotes

'When the time comes – it's no good carving it up.' (Nugget: p.22)

'It's my family's farm.' (William: p.32)

'...this bloody farm has been a noose around her neck for sixty years.' (William: p.37)

'You've got to be big to own country like this.' (Farley: p.41)

'One of us takes on the farm and the other is free to go ... Right?' (Young Girlie: p.48)

'We have to make a decision about the farm. My children need to know where they stand.' (Girlie: p.52)

'... she [Jessie Allan] didn't call it Allandale so some freeloader could just walk in.' (Girlie: p.55)

'It's a question of blood. Allandale belongs to Lyle.' (Girlie: p.57)

To 'inherit' means to acquire property by legal succession, or to be the recipient of a genetic or hereditary characteristic. Both these meanings of 'inheritance' operate in the play. In terms of land ownership, there are conflicting and competing rights, as the claims of those who work the land jostle with those who have a 'spiritual' connection and ancestral claims, and those whose rights are recognised by the law. The characters who consider themselves to be the rightful inheritors of Allandale have one or more of these reasons for making a claim.

Inherited qualities or characteristics, such as the depressive predisposition Lyle inherits from his grandfather, Norm Myrtle, also play a key role in determining the course of one's life. Hereditary qualities are closely connected with the notion of fate. These are played out through the character of Lyle, who shares Norm's passion for pigeons, echoes his pessimistic sentiments – 'Life is not fair' (pp.31, 34) – and inevitably repeats his tragic fate.

Inheritance of property or money is usually beneficial, but it can also be seen as a burden – as Rayson's characters demonstrate. Dibs sacrifices her dreams of a career in Melbourne, accepting the 'flip of a coin' as a sign of her destiny. William's assertion that the farm has been 'a noose around her neck for sixty years' (p.37) highlights the heavy burden that is part of an inheritance: it is Girlie, who doesn't inherit the farm, who is 'free to go' (p.48).

Relationship with the land – or belonging

Key quotes

'Mate, the land belongs to the people who work it.' (Maureen: p.32)

'This is Nugget's country. His people have already been dispossessed once. He has a spiritual attachment to this place.' (Felix: p.91)

'Dad could tell you every tree, every hill. Every creek. We belong here too.' (Brianna: p.91)

Questions of ownership jostle with questions of belonging, and the play demonstrates that there is often a moral dimension which undercuts legal entitlement to property ownership. Nugget's rights are endorsed by the play, and also by Farley, but legal rights ultimately prevail – and perpetuate the injustices perpetrated on Nugget's ancestors.

Rural/urban divide

Key quotes

'And like this is where it's really happening.' (Felix: p.12)

'How are you, mate? Still a real asphalt fella. Eh?' (Nugget: p.20)

'Fokaishas. See! We're up with it.' (Dibs: p.26)

'The Rushton A & P ... was the only exciting thing that ever happened in this shit-heap.' (William: p.23)

'It's bad luck, that place [Melbourne].' (Girlie: p.29)

'They're thieves down there – the builders and that. They'll see you coming a mile off.' (Girlie: p.54)

'We live in a ghetto ... We all think the same, but out here – they hate blacks, they hate wogs. They hate brown people.' (Felix: p.83)

'Because you're from the city, you think you know everything. It's a big joke out this way.' (Maureen: p.85)

'Dibs: He's a vegan, apparently.

Girlie: What? From Venus?' (p.90)

The city, to many of the characters, seems sophisticated and full of promise: for young Dibs Hamilton the city represents 'everything [she] always dreamed of' (p.48); a place where she can pursue a career and escape from the burden of her inheritance. William and Julia also escaped from the country – with its limited opportunities and its culture of homophobia.

By contrast, the country can seem parochial and uncivilised. Country life is often unglamorous – with its mouse plagues, droughts and small-town gossip. Characters such as Ashleigh, Felix and William regard the country as a dull, provincial 'shit-heap' (p.23) where you 'wait for something to happen' (p.12). Rayson herself stresses that there is nothing idyllic about the play, the tone of which is marked by desperation and violence.[25] To those who do appreciate it, however, the country offers a 'spiritual' connection with the land (p.91). The romanticisation of the country by characters like Julia is connected with a notion that city life is stressful and almost dehumanising. Girlie also prefers the country, believing that the city is dangerously polluted and this is a by-product of its sophistication. She believes that the city is 'bad luck' and that the 'gin slings', 'big orchestra' and Collins Street boutiques can come at a high price (p.29). Girlie's sojourn in the city results in 'nine months cooped up in the Alfred Hospital' suffering from polio and Norm's pigeon returns to the country, having been bought by 'a bloke in the city' who got tuberculosis and went 'into a sanatorium' (p.29).

Cultural differences between country and city are highlighted by William's contributions to the party menu: 'Chicken wings with soy sauce

---

[25] Usher, 'Hannie's outback odyssey'.

and sesame seeds' (p.25), 'Asparagus and prosciutto parcels ... zucchini and goat's cheese pizzas' (p.26). Dibs' mispronunciation of 'fokaishas' (p.26) reinforces William's (and perhaps the audience's) perceptions of 'unsophisticated' country people. By contrast, plain and hearty country cooking includes 'cream horns ... ginger fluffs, asparagus rolls, lamingtons, cheese boats' (p.19). This almost iconic country fare evokes a long-past era, when culinary skills were the measure of womanhood just as mechanical expertise (such as Lyle's) was the measure of a man. Country food also reflects the simple tastes of the down-to-earth people who produce the raw ingredients. City food is more complex and more likely to involve exotic ingredients and complicated recipes, and it can veer towards being pretentious. Food preparation in the city has moved beyond the female and domestic realm to include professional restaurateurs – such as William.

Q Is there an element of condescension in urban attitudes to country life?

Q On what grounds might city people consider themselves superior, and does Rayson implicitly agree with the urban perspective?

Financial hardship

Key quotes

'There's people in this town can't afford a raffle ticket.' (Girlie: p.15)

'I'm putting in a sixty-hour week – for what? We're going down the toilet ...' (Maureen: p.25)

'Put [the pigeons] in a sack and drown them in the river. We can't afford to keep pigeons.' (Maureen: p.25)

'Poor Dad. It was all too hard, trying to scratch a living ... he was doing every dead-end job he could get.' (Dibs: p.26)

The Delaneys' precarious economic situation is typical of many small farmers hit by the rural recession and constantly beset by natural disasters. Maureen informs Lyle that 'there's not enough money in the cheque book' to pay the gas bill and that they cannot even afford for their daughters to 'go to the pictures' (p.24). Despite this, Lyle wants to buy a 'three-tonne seeder' and Girlie encourages him, enquiring whether Jack Cummins is selling. This infuriates Maureen, who 'treks off to Swan Hill every bloody day to work in that shop' (p.24). Maureen's distress is fuelled by her expectation that men – in particular, her husband – should earn sufficient to '[keep] this family together' (p.24). Lyle, however, is unable to face up to the grim reality of their economic circumstances.

As she and Girlie sit outside the Rushton CFA collecting signatures for a petition to establish a rural transaction centre, Maureen draws attention to pressing rural issues: bank and post-office closures. This increases the economic hardship for local traders because Rushton residents now find it more convenient to shop in Swan Hill, a large regional centre (p.46). Motivated by her concern over local issues, Maureen is 'going into politics' (p.47). The National Party, which previously could have endorsed 'a chook' and local people 'woulda voted for it' (p.47), is rapidly losing its traditional supporter base. Independents such as Maureen Delaney, who have a strong, personal connection with country dwellers, suddenly become a political force.

Family conflict

Key quotes

'See Lyle and me, we don't see eye-to-eye on this.' (Nugget: p.21)

'Nobody's forcing you to stick around.' (Lyle to Maureen: p.25)

'This is not fair, Dibs – what you're doing.' (Girlie: p.51)

'You didn't bother to say anything to us. Your own family.' (Girlie: p.52)

'This is a matter for family, I'm afraid.' (Girlie: p.55)

'Freeloader? What's got into you?' (Dibs: p.55)

'Our mother did what you [Dibs] told her ... she signed over everything –' (Girlie: p.57)

'Get in the car. And don't come back.' (Maureen: p.92)

The battle for possession of Allandale tears the two families apart. The Hamiltons and the Delaneys bicker with each other and among themselves: Julia, Felix and William argue; Maureen and Lyle become increasingly hostile and Maureen eventually orders Lyle to leave. Dibs and Girlie's close relationship shows signs of stress as they are drawn into the conflict. Most disturbingly, however, Lyle and Nugget, who 'used to be mates' (p.83), have a 'vicious and frightening' fight (pp.57–8).

Q Family conflict often arises around the issue of how best to care for ageing and infirm parents. What cultural, social and personal values might influence such decisions? Do different values operate in different cultures?

Discrimination/intolerance and values

Racism

Key quotes

'Dibs [has] gone and asked the wogs.' (Girlie: p.13)

'They're thieves, those Greeks!' (Girlie: p.15)

'White teacher living with a blackfella. Even the kids in her class were having a go at her.' (Nugget: p.20)

'Bloody boong. Never had to stand on your own two feet, you black bastard.' (Lyle: p.44)

'I'm talking about every Asian, Moslem and Hottentot who come here and refuse to sign up to the Australian Way of Life.' (Maureen: p.61)

'... some little Asiatic nurse is scrubbing you down with kerosene.' (Girlie: p.53)

'Then why didn't you choose a proper man?' (Dibs: p.70)

Homophobia

Key quotes

'Gay men are not welcome in Rushton.' (William: p.10)

'Well, nobody need know. He doesn't have to advertise the fact.' (Dibs: p.10)

'I thought he [Felix] was a homo.' (Maureen: p.15)

'I just don't like to think about it.' (Nugget, referring to William and Kevin's relationship: p.20)

'Obviously there are people in this world who can't overcome their own ... weakness.' (Farley, to William: p.23)

Religious intolerance

Key quotes

'It's the Presbyterian in her [Dibs]. Stingy.' (Girlie: p.15)

'You can't fight those Presbyterian sheilas.' (Lucky Joe: p.42)

'Never put a Mick in charge of anything.' (Farley: p.43)

'You can tell a Catholic by his eyes.' (Norm, recalled by Young Dibs: p.48)

'She's a Christian. They do all sorts of weird shit.' (Felix: p.67)

We are all shaped by the values of our society and gradually develop our own set of beliefs and standards in response to these values. The play reveals the ways in which we inherit values: from our parents, our religion, our socio-economic and cultural groups. These values become part of our identity and we often defend them passionately.

Often when the strongly held values of diverse individuals and groups come into conflict, prejudice, vilification and exclusion are utilised by the culturally dominant group against less powerful minorities: in rural Rushton, these minority groups are migrants, Catholics, Aboriginal people and homosexuals.

Key point

In a play where no-one is untainted by prejudice, Rayson makes us aware of the fine line between defending one's own values and condemning, often unfairly, the values of others.

Q Does discriminatory language (terms such as 'pansy', 'fairy', 'faggot', 'coon', 'boong', 'wog' and 'Mick') play a significant role in perpetuating prejudice?

Q Is remaining silent in the face of prejudiced opinions a way of condoning and perpetuating prejudice?

Q Is tolerance of cultural difference simply a trendy, middle-class fashion?

Q Is there a deeply entrenched homophobia embedded in the relatively common (derogatory) use of the word 'gay' (as in: 'that's so gay')?

Q Why are there such enduring cultural taboos connected with interracial sex? Why do these taboos operate more strongly when a black man and a white woman are involved?

Q Traditional rivalries between Catholics and Protestants, arising from our convict past, have shaped Australian society. We are largely incapable of accepting those who are different. Do you agree?

Q Do the sons of migrant families need to rely on sporting skills, particularly on the football field, to gain acceptance in Australia?

Gender

Key quotes

'Sweetheart. You need to create a bit of mystery.' (Maureen: p.28)

'You weak little git.' (Farley to Felix: p.40)

'What's with all the Nobbys and Dongers?' (Felix: p.64)

'She's making that boy of hers a bloody wuss ...' (Girlie: p.90)

Femininity

Traditional attitudes to the feminine are encapsulated in the Myrtle twins' song in the prologue, 'Two Little Girls in Blue' (p.2), a sentimental popular song of the era which constructs the feminine ideal as childlike and therefore sexually innocent. The 'two little girls' are constructed by the 'gaze' of the male subject, who eventually sexually initiates one of the girls. Maureen's advice to Ashleigh about needing to leave something 'to the imagination' (p.28) effectively acknowledges the male gaze and encourages her adolescent daughter's compliance in becoming a passive object of sexual desire, thus implicitly supporting the perpetuation of gender stereotyping.

As the two little Myrtle girls negotiate womanhood in a changing social landscape, Dibs is forced by circumstances to exercise the patriarchal power bequeathed to her by her father, Norm. She ultimately utilises her power to dispossess Nugget, just as her colonising ancestors had dispossessed Nugget's Aboriginal ancestors. Maureen's circumstances require her to move beyond an entirely domestic role. However, she deeply resents travelling to Swan Hill every day 'to work in that shop' (p.24). Julia challenges gender stereotyping by climbing the career ladder in the Multicultural Commission and acquires basic car-repair skills, yet she yearns to abandon her career for a return to a maternal and domestic role.

Thus, while Rayson's female characters are often empowered by questioning traditional female roles and moving beyond stereotypes, she does not assume that there are unproblematic solutions for women who challenge patriarchal values.

Masculinity

Rayson also examines traditional notions of masculinity and the often catastrophic effects of unquestioning adherence to them. Many such qualities are embodied in Lyle Delaney: he is a 'good farmer' (p.25), physically strong and skilled with his hands. Lyle's conversion of a lawnmower into a motorbike for Girlie provides a deliberate contrast with city-born Felix, who is perversely proud of his mechanical incompetence and cannot tell the difference between a spanner and a screwdriver (p.4). On the other hand, Lucky Joe Delaney epitomises traditional notions of masculinity. Described by Nugget as a 'good bloke', he allegedly 'won the Stawell Gift' (p.43). Ruggedly heterosexual, athletic and enterprising, Lucky Joe is universally admired.

The existence of a 'macho' subculture which celebrates sporting ability and (hetero)sexual prowess is also evident in the nicknames of the local boys, mostly well-endowed footballers with names like 'Nobby', 'Donger' and 'Horny'. 'Horse Horrigan', who 'had a whopper' (p.64), acquired local hero status. On a more sober note, adherence to gender stereotypes ultimately defeats men like Lyle, whose failure to provide for his family implies his unmanliness. In Maureen's eyes he is a 'useless idiot' and a 'hopeless piece of trash' (p.73), and his suicide can be seen as an escape from the disgrace of financial ruin. Rayson also demonstrates that traditional notions of masculinity are no longer appropriate, in that they exclude men such as William and Felix.

Role reversals

Rayson's examination of gender stereotypes involves some comic role reversals. In Act one, scene one, it is Julia who 'examines things' (p.3) under the car bonnet, while Felix 'squints into the distance', proclaiming that he 'hate[s] cars' (p.3). A more problematic reversal of gender roles occurs in Lyle and Maureen's relationship. While Maureen's adoption of the traditional 'male' roles of breadwinner and social activist might seem liberating, her bitterness at the need to do so reveals a deeply ingrained adherence to gender stereotypes.

Nevertheless, Maureen's acquisition of political power (displacing the long-standing male candidate) endorses a role for women beyond the domestic and maternal spheres assigned to them by their social and biological inheritance. However, patriarchal power, whether in the hands of men or women, and even when it seems benign, is always oppressive because of the way it creates hierarchies.

Q Are overt displays of homophobia an integral part of male-bonding rituals?

Q Are there equivalent rituals among women?

Binary oppositions

Binary oppositions are pairs of terms that seek to create 'mutually exclusive' categories. Some of the oppositions in *Inheritance* are:

freedom	duty
black Australians	white Australians
inheritance	dispossession
heterosexuality	homosexuality
country	city
tolerance	prejudice
youth	age
legal rights	moral rights
present	past
Catholic	Protestant
Anglo-Saxon	non–Anglo-Saxon
fate	individual responsibility

Binary oppositions underpin the ideology of a patriarchal society, in that they seek not only to categorise, but also to create hierarchies, whereby cultural values or groups of people on one side of a 'dividing line' are approved (by majority consent), while those on the other side are not.

Q Find examples of ways in which the text challenges traditional assumptions connected with binary oppositions. Each of these sets of oppositions can be developed as a theme. You should make a chart, collect quotations and find (or devise your own) essay topics which ask you to explore the text by looking carefully at these sets of binary oppositions. When the binary oppositions in this play are closely examined, they are not always mutually exclusive. Where and why have they been merged?

QUESTIONS & ANSWERS

The essay topics below show a range of possible styles and formats, and are suitable for senior English assessment tasks and examinations.

Essay topics

1. "Don't you ever call me coon."
   'The unresolved tension between Lyle and Nugget is more about racial prejudice than farming.'
   Discuss.
2. "You put in the work and you get your rewards."
   'Lyle Delaney is the rightful heir to Allandale.'
   Do you agree?
3. "You won this farm on the flip of a coin."
   'Dibs's and Girlie's flip of the coin ultimately destroys their families.'
   Discuss.
4. "Who says life is fair? Life is not fair."
   In what ways is life 'not fair' to Lyle Delaney?
5. "This is not about what's good for you."
   'The characters in the play are all equally greedy and selfish.'
   Do you agree?
6. "He had a proper home … and proper schooling."
   'Dibs and Farley do the right thing in bringing Nugget up as their son.'
   Discuss.
7. "This farm stays in the family. It's a question of blood."
   'The text shows that even the strongest family relationships are threatened by questions of inheritance.'
   Discuss.

8 "You weak little git."
'*Inheritance* shows that those who do not measure up to society's expectations are rejected.'
Discuss.

9 "You know who he reminds me of? Lyle Delaney."
'*Inheritance* shows that the actions of the past determine the course of our lives.'
Discuss.

10 "Because you're from the city, you think you know everything."
'*Inheritance* shows that city and country dwellers will never understand each other.'
Discuss.

11 "Your generation is just soft."
'*Inheritance* shows that intergenerational conflict is an inevitable part of family relationships.'
Discuss.

12 "... this bloody farm has been a noose around her neck for sixty years."
'The text shows that inheritance is both a curse and a blessing.'
Discuss.

Analysing a sample topic

"This farm stays in the family. It's a question of blood."
'The text shows that even the strongest family relationships are threatened by questions of inheritance.' Discuss.

- Taking the topic apart is the key to a successful text response. The topic makes an assertion about the text, which you might or might not agree with – or you might agree with some of it.
- This topic asks you to agree with the assertion that, in the play, money and property are shown to be more important than people. Is this true? Think about the relationships in the play: husbands and wives, parents and children, siblings, cousins.
- Which are the strongest relationships? (What does 'strongest' mean here?) Are they 'threatened'? How? Are they threatened by things other than inheritance? This brainstorming will provide you with discussion points which may become useful topic sentences for your paragraphs.
- Make a list of all the relationships that are threatened by disagreements about who will inherit Allandale. (Are there any that are not threatened – or even some that are strengthened?) Of those that are threatened, list all the factors which put pressure on them: if they survive, why do they?
- Gather quotes and evidence to support your assertion about the text (which may not agree entirely with the topic's assertion). You can say 'yes' (I completely agree with the topic); 'yes, but …' (there is something I don't quite agree with); 'no' (I totally disagree) or 'no, but …' (I mostly disagree with it).
- Another useful strategy is to think about this as an 'either/or' topic: either families, or money and property, are important to people. You are then free to disagree with this and say that both are important. An 'either/or' position can be turned into an 'as well as' or even a 'because of' position. For example, it could be argued that it is only

because of the importance of family that money and property matter – because they provide security. This might be a useful discussion point to develop in one of your paragraphs.

- Now you are ready to show your thinking about the topic – and to make your own assertion in your introduction. You should also take into account the broader implications of the idea of inheritance.
- Ask questions about what kinds of things – apart from property – can be thought of as part of an inheritance. Lyle inherits some of Norm's depressive tendencies, but more significantly, prejudices and values are inherited as they are passed from generation to generation.
- You could also think about the way that some people do not inherit what is rightfully theirs. In this play it is Nugget who is disinherited and who represents his disinherited people.
- Connecting the idea of Aboriginal disinheritance to the topic – which asks you to look at family tensions – might also lead you to reflect that society has been destabilised by the dispossession of Aboriginal people.
- Here's a sample introduction:

  Family relationships in *Inheritance* are destabilised by unresolved questions about who will inherit Allandale. Relationships already under pressure as a result of financial hardship deteriorate rapidly, as the impending death of Farley Hamilton propels the issue of Allandale's inheritance into the foreground. Friendly relationships turn sour and degenerate into bitter animosity. Even strong relationships are unsettled by conflicting beliefs about Allandale's rightful heir. Although other factors, such as greed, selfishness and racial prejudice, also threaten family relationships, it could be argued that these issues arise as a consequence of disputes about inheritance. The battle for ownership of Allandale also raises larger questions about who 'owns' Australia, and how we resolve disputes about land rights claims.

- As you construct your response, you should draw on your thinking about the topic, as this will provide you with an argument. Each of your paragraphs should begin with a clear but subtle reference to back your assertion about the topic. In each paragraph, you need to draw on a range of quotes and specific textual references to support your assertions about theme and character.
- Your conclusion should not simply reiterate your introduction or summarise your main points. You should remind the reader of your contention about the topic and it is sometimes useful to remind the reader of a point you have already made in the essay about the cultural and political values embedded in the text.
- Finally, try to demonstrate not only your understanding, but also your enjoyment of the text.

SAMPLE ANSWER

'*Inheritance* demonstrates that families can be torn apart through disloyalty and betrayal.' Discuss.

Inheritance is a play about the disintegration of family relationships. The Hamiltons and the Delaneys are ultimately torn apart by disloyalty and betrayal. However, the play also shows that even in the midst of the most bitter family breakdown, some individuals will rally to support those damaged by treachery or duplicity.

Disloyalty and betrayal irrevocably damage most of the relationships in *Inheritance*. As Farley Hamilton becomes increasingly frail and incompetent, the once harmonious relationship between the Myrtle sisters begins to unravel. Girlie feels betrayed by the fact that Dibs has not consulted her on the sale of the farm. She also accuses Dibs of betraying Jessie Allen, their grandmother, who cleared the land and would not want 'some freeloader' to 'just walk in'. This is a spiteful reference to Farley, whose name on the title means 'bugger all' to Girlie. Her angry denunciation of Farley's right to name an heir is an implicit criticism of Dibs, whose support of Farley is seen as the betrayal of a deeper loyalty owed to the descendants of the Myrtle family.

The prophetic words of the song 'Two Little Girls in Blue' foreshadow the way in which 'destiny' will draw the Myrtle twins apart. As Girlie begins to question the validity of a bargain made 'on the flip of a coin', her loyalty to her sister, whose husband has made a 'damn good living' from Allandale, wavers. She confronts Dibs, insisting that their agreement is 'not binding' on the next generation. Girlie's resentment of the Hamiltons is only exceeded by Maureen's, whose family is plunging into debt. Unable to maintain her loyalty to a husband she regards as a 'hopeless piece of trash', Maureen directs her fury towards the Hamiltons, whose 'private school voices' and 'period furniture' sharpen the edge of the Delaneys' poverty and reinforce their prejudices about 'pampered' city dwellers who have, in their view, forfeited their right to inherit the farm.

Exacerbating the atmosphere of treachery in the family is Lyle Delaney's shameful betrayal of a 'mate'. As the effects of drought begin to hit hard, Lyle and Nugget disagree about farm management. Lyle arrogantly dismisses Nugget's advice, claiming that his Diploma of Agriculture is 'not worth the paper [it's] printed on'. Felix accuses Lyle of being unable to accept 'that an Aborigine'd have ideas', confronting Lyle with the unpleasant truth of his racism. Compounding his racial prejudice, Lyle is driven by a need to be his 'own boss' and is angered by Nugget's refusal to 'go halves' in a three-tonne seeder. Lyle takes out a loan to pay for the seeder, and when the bank demands repayment, Lyle convinces himself that Nugget 'backed out' of the deal. Lyle's desperation turns to rage and he vents his frustration on Nugget, screaming racist abuse and physically attacking him in a 'vicious and frightening' fight. This shocking violence brings to the surface the simmering tensions that are tearing the family apart.

The disloyalty to and betrayal of Nugget are at the heart of the family conflict. Farley betrays Nugget by refusing to officially acknowledge his paternity. Farley's inability to 'tell them the truth' leaves Nugget without a 'leg to stand on' when Dibs rips up Farley's will. Dibs' bitterness surfaces after Farley's death, and in leaving the farm to Lyle she takes her revenge on the husband who betrayed her and on his 'bastard son'. Girlie is complicit in this act of betrayal, insisting that Dibs has 'done the right thing'. The 'legal and proper' document that transfers the property to Lyle is a shameful reminder of the ruthless dispossession of Nugget's ancestors by white colonisers. Rayson's play draws clear parallels with Australian society, still bitterly divided in the wake of the betrayal of Indigenous Australians, whose land was forcefully acquired and whose children were unwillingly assimilated into white society.

While relationships in the Hamilton and Delaney families are eroded by disloyalty and betrayal, not everyone is disloyal. As financial problems drive Lyle to drink and desperation and his wife denounces him as 'a loser', Girlie remains steadfastly loyal. Brianna also staunchly defends her father. She explains to Felix: 'whatever decision [he] makes ... doesn't work out. But it's not his fault'. Brianna and Lyle are united by their love of pigeons and their 'spiritual' connection to the land, and her faith in Lyle might have restored his faith in himself. Tragically, however, Brianna's loyalty is not enough. Lyle's misplaced trust in the bank's integrity is shattered by a visit from the bailiff, and his deep sense of betrayal finally seals his fate. Like his grandfather, Norm Myrtle, Lyle succumbs to despair.

The breakdown of relationships in the Hamilton and Delaney families reveals the devastating consequences of betrayal and disloyalty. The two families are driven apart as tensions erupt into violence, and the abrupt blackout as the play ends suggests that there is little hope of reconciliation.

REFERENCES & READING

The text

Rayson, Hannie, *Inheritance,* Currency Press, Sydney, 2003.

There are two editions of *Inheritance*, both published by Currency Press in 2003: the MTC edition, containing the script only, and an edition that also contains a very useful discussion of the play by dramaturg Hilary Glow, and a 'Director's note' by Simon Phillips, who directed the MTC's 2003 season. I recommend the latter and the page references in this Text Guide refer to this edition.

Books

O'Reilly, Christopher, *Context in Literature: Post Colonial Literature,* Cambridge University Press, Cambridge, 2001.

Peck, John & Coyle, Martin, *Literary Terms and Criticism*, Macmillan, London, 1984.

Newspaper articles and author interviews

Adams, Phillip, *The Weekend Australian Magazine*, 23–4 July 2005, p.46.

Glow, Hilary, 'Class action', *Meanjin*, Vol. 64, Nos. 1&2, 2005, pp.326–35.

Usher, Robin, 'Hannie's outback odyssey', *The Age*, 21 February 2003, The Culture p.3.

Websites

Darracott, Rosalyn, 'Applying a grief model to working with pastoralists', National Rural Health Alliance, 2003, https://eprints.qut.edu.au/101410/1/darracott.pdf

Fourth Wall, 2005, Wikipedia, the free encyclopedia, https://en.wikipedia.org/wiki/Fourth_wall

Manne, Robert, 'The stolen generations: Robert Manne's essay', Tim Richardson, 1998, http://tim-richardson.net/index.php/opinion/the-stolen-generations-robert-manne

Papers of Edward Koiki Mabo, National Library of Australia, 2009, https://nla.gov.au/nla.obj-224065802/findingaid

Pauline Hanson, 2005, *Wikipedia*, the free encyclopedia, http://en.wikipedia.org/wiki/Pauline_Hanson

Peckham, Sarah, 'Pauline Hanson & One Nation', Action for Aboriginal Rights, 1998, http://home.vicnet.net.au/~aar/sarah2.htm (no longer available)

Social Development Committee of the Parliament of South Australia, 'Rural poverty in South Australia: interim report of the Social Development Committee', Parliament of South Australia, 1994, http://www.parliament.sa.gov.au/committees/lccdocuments/SD/public_documents/Tabled%20Reports/04th%20Report;%20Interim%20Rural%20Poverty%20Inquiry%20Report.pdf (no longer available)